GREEK
CUISINE
THE NEW CLASSICS

GREEK CUISINE
THE NEW CLASSICS

Peter Conistis

Illustrated by Skye Rogers

TEN SPEED PRESS
Berkeley, California

To Eleni, whose inspiration and dedication to our food have given more to this book than I can say. Thank you.

Text copyright © 1994 Peter Conistis
Illustrations copyright © 1994 Skye Rogers

A Kirsty Melville book.

1☯

TEN SPEED PRESS
P.O. Box 7123
Berkeley, CA 94707

First published in Australasia in 1994 by
Simon & Schuster Australia
20 Barcoo Street, East Roseville NSW 2069

A Paramount Communications Company
Sydney New York London Toronto Tokyo Singapore

Text designed by Helen Semmler
Additional design work by Michelle Havenstein
Illustrations by Skye Rogers
Typeset in Australia by Asset Typesetting Pty Ltd

Library of Congress Cataloging-in-Publication Data

Conistis, Peter.
    Greek cuisine : the new classics / by Peter Conistis : illustrated
    by Skye Rogers.
        p.   cm.
    Includes index.
    ISBN 0-89815-646-7 : $15.95
    1. Cookery, Greek. I. Title.
TX723.5G8C657 1994
641.59495—dc20   94-13150
                                                            CIP

FIRST PRINTING 1994
Produced by Mandarin Offset
Printed and bound in China
1 2 3 4 5 — 98 97 96 95 94

CONTENTS

INTRODUCTION

IN ANCIENT GREECE, a professional cook was regarded as an artist. When these cooks created new dishes, they were honoured at ceremonies in front of huge gatherings and given titles as rewards, as well as gifts of gold and land. Terion, an Athenian baker, was even mentioned in the writings of Plato and Aristophanes.

In the Middle Ages, many intellectuals found their way into Orthodox monasteries to escape Byzantine overlords. In true Greek tradition, they were fine cooks who donned black robes and created extravagant dishes for the delighted monks who until that time had subsisted on more spartan fare. To distinguish themselves from the monks, they wore tall white hats instead of the black ones worn by their monastic colleagues. To this day, we associate those hats with the master chefs of fine dining restaurants.

Today, Greece, its food and its people promote, in my opinion, a warm sense of hospitality and the ability to live life to its fullest extent. Whether a friend or a stranger is invited to someone's home, something to eat and drink is always offered, even if it is only a small serving of sweetmeats and a cup of strong Greek coffee.

When most people think of Greek food, they think of what they have been served in cheap 'Greek-style' restaurants outside of Greece. Real Greek cuisine is nothing like that. It's honest food — simple and flavourful. Much of what is eaten is tied to the seasons: artichokes and broad (fava) beans in spring; tomatoes, zucchini (courgettes) and eggplant (aubergines) in summer; legumes and root vegetables in winter.

Greek cuisine is also very regional in nature. In the far north, Pontian Greeks have a cuisine all their own and are skilful hands at pickling. Staples in their cooking are leeks, cabbages and sardines, fresh and salted.

On the islands, while the cooking is simple peasant fare, their cuisine has developed through ingenuity due to the few resources available and the scarcity of agricultural land. The Ionian Islands, however, are a much more cultivated group. Their influences reflect those of the Italian and Venetian explorers of the past, claiming dishes with very un-Greek names such as fish *bianco*, and the Corfiot dishes of *sofrito* and *pastitsatha*, as their own.

Greek meals are eaten in a different progression than many people are used to. One large meal is served in the middle of the day. This routine means that Greeks have become known as great snackers. Most people start their day with a couple of *koulouria* (sesame rings) from the corner vendor. Throughout the day they will drink copious amounts of strong coffee and snack on cheese or spinach pies, various sweet and savoury pastries, small bags of salted pistachio nuts, pumpkin seeds (pepitas) or roasted chickpeas to keep them going until lunch.

All shops, museums, theatres and offices close around 1 o'clock and everyone goes home for a large lunch and siesta. Refreshed, most Greeks go back to work around 4 o'clock and work until 8 or 9 o'clock at night. This means that dinner is served later than in many cultures. It is always a lighter meal, many times enjoyed at the local taverna or *ouzerie* as a plate *mezethes* and a few glasses of ouzo or wine. Ah! What a life!

At my restaurant, Cosmos, I have tried to take this classic approach to Greek food and adapt it to the lifestyle I have grown up and lived with here in Australia. By relying on the best local seasonal ingredients (some of which are not part of the traditional Greek diet) and my need to re-create, explore and rework traditional recipes (many now forgotten by most Greek cooks), I always aim for my food to evoke that feeling of freshness, simplicity and balance that I have grown up with, knowing and appreciating Greek cuisine as I do.

MEZETHES AND APPETISERS

IN SUMMER, TINY TAVERNAS throughout Greece are swamped with people — people sipping shot glasses of ouzo or long glasses of cold lager, and the same people nibbling on an array of small plates of *mezethes*. *Mezethes* is usually translated as 'appetiser' or 'starter', but this translation does not do justice to the fundamental role *mezethes* play in Greek tradition.

History notes that Ancient Greeks made it impossible for their society to indulge in alcohol without some tasty morsel to nibble on. They knew that drinking on an empty stomach was not a sensible idea, so it became mandatory to serve *mezethes* wherever and whenever alcohol was offered. Since then *mezethes* have become an integral part of Greek social life.

Mezethes can take the form of something as humble as a few olives, a small piece of cheese and some fresh, crisp radishes all the way through to platters laden with different dips, tiny skewers of grilled lamb or pork, deep-fried squid or whitebait (smelt) and little savoury filo triangles or rolls.

Mezethes are served everywhere in Greece, throughout every season of the year, and are one of the most enjoyable features of Greek cuisine. With this in mind, these are some of the appetisers I have developed at my restaurant.

CHICKPEA BOUREKIA

Bourekia me Revithia

250 g (8 oz) cooked chickpeas
2 tablespoons virgin olive oil
1 onion, finely chopped
1 clove garlic, finely chopped
2 tomatoes, peeled, seeded and
   finely chopped
salt and freshly ground black
   pepper, to taste
½ cup (125 mL/4 fl oz) dry white
   wine
125 g (4 oz) goat's milk or other
   feta cheese, crumbled
1 tablespoon finely chopped fresh
   coriander (cilantro)
1 egg, beaten
225 g (7 oz) filo pastry
olive oil, as needed

Serves 6 as part of a mezethes
   plate

BOUREKIA ARE FILO pastry rolls which are generally made with a cheese or spicy meat filling. These are a variation on the ones I tried on the island of Samos, which were made without the usual cheese and egg as it was during Lent, but were still delicious.

Preheat the oven to 190°C (375°F/gas mark 5).

Mash the chickpeas in a large bowl and set aside. Cook the olive oil, onion and garlic in a saucepan, until the onion and garlic are translucent. Add the tomatoes, salt and pepper, and stir. Now add the wine and cook for 5 minutes. Remove from the heat. When the mixture has cooled, stir in the cheese, chickpeas, coriander and egg. Adjust seasoning if necessary. Set aside.

Now prepare the pastry. Cut the filo pastry into rectangles about 10 cm x 20 cm (4 in. x 8 in.). Brush each sheet with a little olive oil. Put a tablespoonful of filling at one end of a sheet. Fold over the sides and nearest end of the filo and roll the pastry lengthways into a sausage shape. Bake for 15–20 minutes, until golden in colour.

BRAISED CHICKEN GIBLETS WITH CUMIN AND GARLIC

Entosthia Kotisia me Kimino ke Skordo

*500 g (1 lb) chicken giblets
(gizzard), trimmed and cleaned*
*4 cups (1 L/1¾ imp. pts) light
chicken stock*
100 mL (3 fl oz) virgin olive oil
1 onion, finely chopped
6 cloves garlic, finely chopped
*1 teaspoon cumin seeds, dry
roasted and ground in a spice
mill*
1 teaspoon dried oregano
100 mL (3 fl oz) dry white wine
*225 mL (7 fl oz) chicken stock,
reserved from poaching*
*salt and freshly ground black
pepper, to taste*

Serves 6 as part of a mezethes
plate

CHICKEN GIBLETS ARE one of my favourite dishes. If braised slowly, as in this recipe, they are irresistible. I occasionally serve these as part of a *mezethes* plate at my restaurant.

Put the giblets and stock into a large saucepan. Bring slowly to the boil. Simmer gently for 60 minutes, then drain the giblets. Reserve the stock.

Place the olive oil, onion and garlic in a large frying pan or skillet. Cook over a low heat for 10 minutes. Add the giblets, cumin and oregano. Stir for 1 minute. Increase the heat and add the wine. When the wine has evaporated, add the reserved stock, salt and pepper. Reduce the heat and simmer for about 30 minutes, until a thick sauce forms in the pan. Serve hot.

PICKLED STUFFED BABY EGGPLANT
Melitzanakia Yemista Toursi

PICKLE SOLUTION
725 mL (23 fl oz) white wine
vinegar
475 mL (15 fl oz) water
2 tablespoons salt
1 teaspoon whole allspice
6 cloves
1 tablespoon black peppercorns
3 tablespoons clear honey

STUFFED BABY EGGPLANT
1 kg (2 lb) baby (Italian) eggplant
(aubergines)
3 medium carrots, peeled and
finely chopped
5 cloves garlic, finely chopped
handful of fresh flat-leaf (Italian)
parsley, finely chopped
1 tablespoon finely chopped fresh
coriander (cilantro)
¾ teaspoon red pepper flakes
stalks of 1 bunch of fresh coriander
(cilantro), blanched in boiling
water for 1 minute, then
refreshed in cold water
3 bay leaves
1 red chilli pepper, cut into 3 slices
olive oil, as needed

Serve as part of a mezethes *plate*

THESE PICKLES ARE an end-of-summer treat for me, made when baby eggplant (aubergines) appear in the markets. If you're lucky, you will find these baby eggplant in Greek or Middle Eastern fruit markets. Otherwise, use small Japanese eggplant, no more than 10 cm (4 in.) in length.

Pickle Solution: Boil the ingredients in a stainless steel saucepan for 10 minutes. Allow to cool completely.

Stuffed Baby Eggplant: Bring boiling, salted water to the boil for blanching eggplant. Remove stems from eggplant and make a short incision lengthways in each one. Place in the boiling water for 2 minutes. Drain the eggplant completely and allow to cool. Put the carrots, garlic, parsley, coriander and red pepper flakes in a bowl and combine well. Loosely stuff each slit in the eggplant with this filling and tie in place securely using the blanched coriander stalks.

Pack the eggplant upright in three medium-sized preserving (canning) jars, with a bay leaf and slice of chilli in each jar. Pour the pickle solution over the eggplant to cover. Now pour over enough olive oil to form a 2 cm (¾ in.) layer of oil at the top of the jar. Seal and store in a cool, dark place for 2–3 weeks before using.

WHITE BEAN SKORDALIA WITH GRILLED VEGETABLES

Skordalia Apo Fasolia me Lahanika Stin Skara

SKORDALIA

*375 g (12 oz) dried baby lima
    (butter) or cannellini beans*
6 cups (1.5 L/2½ imp. pts) water
pinch of salt
5 cloves garlic, finely chopped
*1 tablespoon finely chopped fresh
    thyme*
*1 cup (250 mL/8 fl oz) extra
    virgin olive oil*
juice of 2 lemons
2 tablespoons grated kefalotyri *or
    mild Parmesan cheese*
freshly ground black pepper, to taste

GRILLED VEGETABLES

*1 medium eggplant (aubergine),
    cut into 1 cm (½ in.) slices*
*3 medium zucchini (courgettes),
    thinly sliced lengthwise*
*1 red capsicum (bell pepper), sliced
    from top to bottom into 6 pieces*
*1 bunch of fresh asparagus,
    trimmed*
extra virgin olive oil, as needed

Serves 6

THIS IS A GREAT DISH to serve at a barbecue as an appetiser or starter; the flavour of the skordalia is really intense and works well with grilled vegetables. Using beans in a skordalia is typical of Northern Greece.

Skordalia: Soak the beans overnight in plenty of cold water. Drain and rinse well. Put the water and salt in a large saucepan. Add the beans and bring to the boil. Cook until the beans have softened.

Place the beans in an electric blender or food processor with the garlic and thyme. Purée until smooth, slowly adding the olive oil and lemon juice as you do so. Add the cheese and continue to process for about 15 seconds. Lastly, add the pepper and adjust seasoning if necessary. Set aside in a serving bowl.

Grilled Vegetables: Salt the eggplant slices and leave for about 30 minutes. Rinse them well and pat dry with a clean cloth. Heat a grill plate or barbecue to very hot. Brush the vegetables with the olive oil and grill on each side for 2–3 minutes. Serve alongside the skordalia.

SALAD OF MARINATED SARDINES, PICKLED EGGPLANT, ROAST TOMATOES AND OLIVES

Salata me Sardeles, Melitzanes, Tomates ke Elies

MARINATED SARDINES
18 sardine fillets, butterflied, with
*   all the bones removed*
sea salt, to taste
juice of 3 lemons
1 teaspoon dried oregano
extra virgin olive oil

PICKLING SOLUTION
2 cups (500 mL/16 fl oz) white
*   wine vinegar*
⅓ cup (100 g/3 oz) sugar
1 teaspoon salt
½ head of garlic, cloves peeled and
*   roughly chopped*
1 bay leaf

PICKLED EGGPLANT
2 medium eggplant (aubergines),
*   thinly sliced lengthways*
salt, to taste
olive oil, for sautéeing

ROAST TOMATOES
¼ cup (60 mL/2 fl oz) olive oil
salt, sugar and freshly ground
*   black pepper, to taste*
6 ripe roma tomatoes, peeled,
*   halved and seeded*
½ teaspoon dried oregano

A GREAT SUMMER SALAD that can also be served as a *mezethes* plate if each part of this dish is served on its own. It needs to be prepared at least 24 hours in advance, but can be made in stages over that time.

Marinated Sardines: Place the sardines in a large, non-corrosive dish and sprinkle generously with sea salt. Add the lemon juice, oregano and enough oil to cover the fillets. Cover and refrigerate for at least 12 hours.

Pickling Solution: Place all the pickling ingredients in a saucepan and bring to the boil. Simmer for 10 minutes. Remove from the heat and allow to cool.

Pickled Eggplant: Sprinkle the eggplant slices generously with salt. Allow to stand for 2 hours to disgorge the bitter juices. Rinse the salt off the eggplant slices and pat them dry with a clean cloth.

Heat some olive oil in a large frying pan or skillet. Sauté the eggplant slices on both sides until they are golden in colour. Drain the eggplant then place in the cold Pickling Solution. Cover and refrigerate for at least 24 hours.

SALAD

150 g (5 oz) kalamata olives,
*   drained and pitted*
1 large handful of young rocket
*   (arugula) leaves*
1 tablespoon small capers, rinsed
*   (salt-preserved capers are best)*

extra virgin olive oil, as needed

Serves 6

Roast Tomatoes: Preheat the oven to 160°C (325°F/ gas mark 3).

Place half the olive oil in a baking dish and sprinkle with the salt, sugar and pepper. Place the tomato halves on top of the oil. Sprinkle over the remaining oil, the oregano and a little more salt, sugar and pepper. Roast for about 20 minutes.

Salad: Gently toss the olives, rocket, capers and tomatoes together.

To Assemble the Dish: Place 2 sardine fillets on each serving plate. Top with some salad, some of the roast tomato, 2 eggplant slices and then some more salad. Finally place another sardine fillet on top. Drizzle with some olive oil.

Alternatively, each of these components can be served separately to make up a *mezethes* platter.

WHITE BEAN SALAD WITH CRAB AND POACHED EGG

Fasolia Salata me Kavouri ke Avgo

300 g (10 oz) dried cannellini beans, soaked overnight in plenty of cold water, drained and rinsed
¼ cup (60 mL/2 fl oz) extra virgin olive oil
2 cloves garlic, minced
large handful of fresh flat-leaf (Italian) parsley, finely chopped
salt and freshly ground black pepper, to taste
300 g (10 oz) spanner or other saltwater crabmeat
1 small sweet white onion, finely chopped
2 tablespoons extra virgin olive oil (extra)
2 tablespoons white wine vinegar
large pinch of salt
6 eggs

Serves 6

IN GREECE, WHITE BEANS are not only used in soups, but are also used as the base of many great salads. This salad, to me, marries the flavours characteristic of Greek cuisine extremely well.

Place the cannellini beans in a large saucepan of cold water. Bring to the boil, simmer for 30 minutes, then cool in the saucepan. Drain.

Mix the beans, olive oil, garlic, parsley, salt and pepper together in a bowl. Set aside and, in another bowl, mix the crabmeat, onion and extra olive oil. Set aside in the refrigerator.

To poach the eggs, bring a large saucepan of water to the boil, add the vinegar and a large pinch of salt. Reduce the heat to a soft boil and break the eggs into the water one at a time. Do not poach all the eggs at once. Have no more eggs in the water at one time than can easily be managed. Poach for about 2 minutes each, remove from the saucepan and refresh in cold water. Drain.

Divide the bean salad among 6 plates. Place some of the crab salad in the centre of each serving of bean salad. Put a poached egg on top of each serving of crab and grind some black pepper over the top of the egg. Serve.

SALAD OF LAMB, ASPARAGUS AND SPRING ONIONS WITH LENTIL AND BLACK OLIVE SALATA

Salata me Arni, Asparagia, Krimidakia kai Eliosalata

LENTIL AND BLACK OLIVE SALATA
150 g (5 oz) brown lentils, rinsed
150 g (5 oz) kalamata olives, pitted
1 tablespoon capers, rinsed (salt-
    preserved capers are best)
1 tablespoon dried Greek
    (Mediterranean) oregano
2 cloves garlic, finely chopped
large handful of fresh flat-leaf
    (Italian) parsley
juice of 1 lemon
freshly cracked black pepper
150 mL (5 fl oz) extra virgin
    olive oil

SALAD
500 g (1 lb) trimmed lamb topside
    or boned loin
1 tablespoon olive oil
freshly cracked black pepper
500 g (1 lb) fresh asparagus,
    trimmed and blanched
1 bunch of spring onions
    (scallions), green tops trimmed,
    blanched for 2 minutes
1 small bunch of watercress, stems
    removed
1 tablespoon Greek Dressing (see
    page 113)

Serves 6

THE LENTIL AND BLACK OLIVE SALATA in this salad makes a fantastic *mezes* on its own, served on slices of toasted bread, or thinned with extra virgin olive oil and used as a dressing over steamed vegetables.

Lentil and Black Olive Salata: Place the lentils in a saucepan. Cover well with cold water. Bring to the boil, reduce the heat and simmer for 45 minutes. Drain and set aside to cool.

When the lentils are cool, place all the ingredients for the salata, except the olive oil, in an electric blender or food processor. Process for 1 minute. With the motor still running, gradually add the oil, as you would when making mayonnaise. Store, refrigerated, in an airtight container.

Salad: Preheat the oven to 220°C (425°F/gas mark 7).

Heat a frying pan or skillet. Roll the lamb in the olive oil and pepper, making sure to season all sides. Quickly brown the meat in the pan — this helps to seal in the juices. Now place the meat in a baking dish and cook in the oven for about 10 minutes. Remove from the oven and leave the lamb to 'rest' for 30 minutes. Do not throw away the juices that have accumulated in the bottom of the dish.

Slice the lamb thinly and place in a bowl with the other salad ingredients (including the juices from the lamb). Toss the lamb gently through the salad.

To serve, place 2 tablespoons of the Lentil and Black Olive Salata on each plate. Divide the salad among the plates, placing on top of the salata. Serve immediately.

COS SALAD WITH PASTOURMAS AND KEFALOTYRI

Salata me Pastourmas, Kefalotiri ke Marouli

*2 baby cos (romaine) lettuces or the
    inner leaves of a large cos lettuce*
1 bunch of rocket (arugula)
9 eggs
*75 g (2½ oz) kefalotyri or mild
    Parmesan cheese, very thinly
    sliced (use a vegetable peeler)*
*30 slices pastourmas (available in
    Greek delicatessens; pastrami
    may be substituted)*
*2 tablespoons stragalia (roasted
    chickpeas), available in Greek
    delicatessens and nut stores*
freshly ground black pepper, to taste
2 tablespoons vinaigrette

Serves 6

I FIRST ATE *PASTOURMAS* when I was about nine years old, and I have been addicted to it ever since. *Pastourmas* is air-dried beef fillets cured with a paprika and garlic paste.

Separate, wash and dry the cos and rocket leaves.

Bring a saucepan of salted water to the boil and gently boil the eggs for 3 minutes. Remove from the heat and refresh in cold water.

Place 5 slices of *pastourmas* in a circle on each serving plate, leaving the centre of the plate free.

Toss the greens with the cheese, *stragalia*, pepper and vinaigrette. Place a small pile of this salad in the centre of each plate. Peel the eggs and slice into halves lengthways. Place 3 halves around each serving of salad. Serve immediately.

ROASTED MUSHROOMS WITH ROCKET AND KEFALOTYRI

Manitaria Psita me Rokka ke Kefalotiri

PINE NUT DRESSING
100 g (3 oz) pine nuts
100 g (3 oz) kefalotyri *or mild*
Parmesan cheese, grated
1 clove garlic, finely chopped
1 tablespoon lemon juice
salt and fresh ground white pepper
½ cup (125 mL/4 fl oz) olive oil
1 tablespoon chilled water

1 kg (2 lb) large field (cultivated)
mushrooms, trimmed and
wiped clean
¼ cup (60 mL/2 fl oz) dressing
(made with 45 mL (1½ fl oz)
extra virgin olive oil, about
½ tablespoon lemon juice and a
pinch of dried oregano)
½ Spanish (red) onion, thinly
sliced into rings
6 handfuls of young rocket
(arugula) leaves, washed and
dried
100 g (3 oz) kefalotyri *or mild*
Parmesan cheese, sliced into
large but thin shavings

Serves 6

KEFALOTYRI IS A HARD CHEESE , commonly made from sheep's milk, but also made with goat's milk. This cheese is dry-salted and left to mature for at least 8 months, and it its best tastes like a good, earthy, Sardinian *sardo*.

Pine Nut Dressing: Process the pine nuts, cheese, garlic, lemon juice, salt and pepper in an electric blender or food processor until smooth. With the motor running, slowly add the olive oil and then the chilled water. Store covered in the refrigerator until needed.

Preheat the oven to 200°C (400°F/gas mark 6). Liberally dress the mushrooms with the olive oil dressing, reserving a little dressing for the salad. Roast the mushrooms on a baking tray (sheet) for 10 minutes.

Toss the onions and rocket in a bowl with the remaining dressing. Arrange the salad on 6 serving plates. Divide the roasted mushrooms among the plates and scatter the shaved cheese over the top. Dress each plate with 2 tablespoons of the Pine Nut Dressing and serve immediately.

KOPANISTI

Kopanisti

1 kg (2 lb) sheep's milk or other
    feta cheese, crumbled
500 g (1 lb) sheep's milk or other
    blue cheese (such as Roquefort),
    crumbled
500 g (1 lb) sheep's milk or other
    ricotta cheese
2 tablespoons sheep's milk or other
    plain yoghurt
1 tablespoon finely chopped fresh
    thyme leaves
1 tablespoon freshly ground black
    pepper
3 tablespoons extra virgin olive oil

Makes about 2 kg (4 lb)

KOPANISTI IS A BLUE CHEESE made with whole sheep's milk, which is coagulated in the same manner as when making feta. However, the coagulation period is longer and the cheese is allowed to ripen for several months before it is ready to eat. This cheese is not readily available outside of Greece. This is the recipe I developed at my restaurant, which we use in a number of guises.

Combine all the ingredients except the olive oil in a large bowl. Slowly pass through a food mill or sieve. Thoroughly fold in the olive oil.

Press into a large plastic container, cover and refrigerate for at least 1 week before serving. This cheese can last for several weeks.

CYPRIOT RAVIOLES IN HALLOUMI, MINT AND BURNT BUTTER SAUCE

Ravioles

250 g (8 oz) halloumi *cheese, rinsed under cold running water to remove excess salt*
2 tablespoons finely shredded fresh mint
¼ teaspoon ground cinnamon
2 eggs
freshly cracked black pepper, to taste
36 gow gee wrappers or won ton skins (available from Asian grocery stores)
100 g (3 oz) unsalted butter
handful of small fresh mint leaves
100 g (3 oz) halloumi *cheese (extra), grated*

Serves 6

THIS CYPRIOT DISH dates back to the Venetian and Genoese occupations of the island during the thirteenth and fourteenth centuries. Traditionally a lenten dish made in great numbers during Carnival Week, now made and enjoyed all year round.

Grate the *halloumi* cheese and mix with the shredded mint, cinnamon, eggs and pepper.

On a large work bench, spread 18 of the wrappers and place a spoonful of the cheese mixture in the centre of each wrapper. Brush a little water around the rim of each wrapper and cover with another wrapper. Press the edges together firmly. Refrigerate for at least 30 minutes.

Bring a large saucepan of salted water to the boil. When boiling, place 6 *ravioles* in the saucepan at a time. When they float to the top, cook for 1 minute longer, then remove from the saucepan and keep warm until all the *ravioles* are cooked.

Divide evenly among 6 entrée plates. Brown the butter in a small pan until sizzling but not burnt. Drop in the mint leaves and stir them through the butter. Pour the butter over the *ravioles* and serve with the extra cheese sprinkled over the top.

'MOUSSAKA' OF EGGPLANT, SEARED SCALLOPS AND TARAMASALATA

Moussaka me Melitzanes, Ktenia ke Taramasalata

TARAMASALATA

3 slices white bread, crusts removed and soaked in some cold water
½ small onion, finely chopped
juice of 1 lemon
100 g (3 oz) smoked gem fish roe (peeled of outer skin) or smoked cod's roe or tarama
225 mL (7 fl oz) extra virgin olive oil

TOMATO SALTSA

2 ripe tomatoes, peeled, seeded and finely chopped
3 tablespoons finely chopped fresh flat-leaf (Italian) parsley
½ teaspoon fennel seeds
2 tablespoons extra virgin olive oil
salt and freshly ground black pepper, to taste

THIS DISH WOULD HAVE TO BE the most popular appetiser or starter we've served at the restaurant. It has been on the menu since day one. The flavours of this layered creation seem to work perfectly. Once again, this dish shows how Greek food blends the flavours of the sea and land so well.

Taramasalata: Place the soaked bread, onion and lemon juice in an electric blender or food processor. Process into a smooth paste, then add the roe and process for a further minute. With the motor still running, slowly add the olive oil, as you would when making mayonnaise. Remove from the blender or processor and chill until needed.

Tomato Saltsa: Combine all the ingredients for the saltsa and chill until needed.

EGGPLANT AND SEARED
SCALLOPS

3 medium eggplants (aubergines),
each cut into 4 circles
salt
vegetable oil for deep-frying
2 red capsicum (bell peppers)
olive oil, as needed
24 white sea scallops
freshly ground black pepper, to taste

Serves 6

Seared Eggplant and Scallops: Sprinkle the eggplant liberally with salt and leave on a tray to sweat for 2 hours. Rinse and dry with a clean cloth to remove any excess moisture. Heat some oil in a deep-fryer or pan. Fry the eggplant slices until golden on both sides. Drain and pat dry on paper towels or absorbent kitchen paper.

Roast the capsicums over a direct flame until their skin blackens. Remove the skin under cold running water. Now remove the pith and seeds, cut the capsicums into strips and mix with a little olive oil.

Heat a frying pan or skillet until 'white' hot. Mix the scallops with a little olive oil and pepper. Place in the pan and sear on each side for 30 seconds. Remove to a plate while preparing each serving.

To Serve: Place a slice of eggplant on each serving plate and dollop 1 tablespoon of Taramasalata on top. Now place 4 scallops on top of the Taramasalata and cover with some strips of the charred capsicum. Cover with another eggplant slice, and finally top with a tablespoon of Tomato Saltsa. Drizzle some of the juices that have collected on the plate holding the scallops around each serving. Serve immediately.

PASTICHIO OF TOMATO NOODLES, LAMB AND SMOKED EGGPLANT

Pastitsio me Arni ke Melitzanes Poure

TOMATO PASTA

*300 g (10 oz) very thin egg noodles
(such as taglierini or tagliatelle)*
*60 g (2 oz) sun-dried tomatoes,
drained and chopped (reserve
the oil)*
2 cloves garlic, finely chopped
*60 g (2 oz) fresh flat-leaf (Italian)
parsley, finely chopped*
*salt and freshly ground black
pepper, to taste*

SMOKED EGGPLANT SALATA

2 medium eggplant (aubergines)
1 small onion, finely chopped
1 clove garlic, finely chopped
½ teaspoon dried oregano
*60 g (2 oz) kefalotyri or mild
Parmesan cheese, grated*
*salt and freshly ground black
pepper, to taste*
*1 tablespoon finely chopped fresh
flat-leaf (Italian) parsley*
*75 mL (2½ fl oz) extra virgin
olive oil*

TRADITIONALLY, *PASTICHIO* IS composed of layers of tubular pasta and a rich lamb sauce, covered with a white cheese sauce and baked to creamy perfection. This traditional dish usually does not make good restaurant fare as it needs to be eaten as soon as it has cooked, and generally in restaurants this is not the case. It is frequently served on holidays, at Sunday dinners or as part of a buffet. Occasionally at Cosmos we serve a special adaptation of *pastichio* where individual servings of flavoured noodles are encased in slow-braised lamb shank meat, cooked in its own sauce, with a layer of smoked eggplant purée replacing the cheese sauce. These are then baked as they are needed — perfect!

Tomato Pasta: Bring a large saucepan of salted water to the boil. Add the noodles and cook as instructed on the packet. When cooked, drain the noodles in a colander and rinse well under cold running water. Set aside in a bowl.

Heat the reserved sun-dried tomato oil in a frying pan or skillet. Add the garlic, sun-dried tomatoes and parsley, and cook over a low heat until the garlic is golden in colour. Add salt and pepper, and then allow the mixture to cool. Toss well in the pasta. Set aside.

Smoked Eggplant Salata: Hold the eggplants over a direct flame or a hotplate until the skins have blackened and blistered on all sides. Cool. Remove the blackened skins and squeeze out the bitter juices and dark seeds. Discard. Place the eggplant in an electric blender or food processor with the remaining ingredients for the salata. Blend or process into a smooth purée. Set aside.

BRAISED LAMB SHANKS
2 tablespoons virgin olive oil
4 lamb shanks, trimmed
1 onion, finely chopped
½ teaspoon cumin seeds, dry-
roasted and ground in a spice
mill
225 mL (7 fl oz) light red wine
(such as Pinot Noir)
1 large tablespoon tomato paste
(purée)
1 cup (250 mL/8 fl oz) rich lamb
or beef stock
salt and freshly ground black
pepper, to taste

ACCOMPANIMENT
Roast Tomato Saltsa (see page 35)

Makes 6 individual serves

Braised Lamb Shanks: Heat the olive oil in a large saucepan. Brown the shanks on all sides, remove from them from the pan and reserve. Leave the oil in the pan and, over a medium heat, cook the onion until it is translucent. Return the shanks to the pan and add the cumin and wine. Cook until the volume of the wine is reduced by half.

Add the tomato paste, stock, salt and pepper. Braise over a low heat for 1–1½ hours, until the lamb comes off the bone easily. Remove the lamb from the saucepan. When cool enough, remove the bones and shred the meat into a bowl. Stir in the pan juices. Adjust the seasoning if necessary.

To Assemble the Dish: Preheat the oven to 200°C (400°F/gas mark 6). Line six 10 cm (4 in.) bread pans or 10 cm (4 in.) pie pans with silicon paper (baking parchment) and lightly oil the paper.

Divide the Tomato Pasta in half and then divide one of these halves evenly among the pans. Reserve the other half for use later. Press the pasta into the corners, covering the bottoms of the pans well. Spread 2 large spoonfuls of the lamb mixture on top of the noodles and then spread 2 large spoonfuls of the eggplant purée over this, making sure you press the mixtures firmly into the pans. Cover the purée with the remaining pasta and then cover each pan with a lid of greased aluminium foil, pressing down firmly and tucking the foil under the rim of the pans.

Bake in the oven for 15 minutes. Carefully remove from the pans and serve immediately, surrounded with Roast Tomato Saltsa.

PRAWNS WITH TOMATO RICE AND SAFFRON

Tomatorizo me Garides ke Krokos

4 tablespoons virgin olive oil
1 onion, finely chopped
3 cloves garlic, finely chopped
3½ cups (500 g/1 lb) short-grain
    rice, preferably arborio
1 kg (2 lb) tomatoes, peeled, seeded
    and chopped
large pinch of saffron threads
salt and freshly ground black
    pepper, to taste
2 cups (500 mL/16 fl oz) light
    chicken stock or water
18 fresh basil leaves, roughly torn
12 green (uncooked) king prawns
    (jumbo shrimp), peeled

Serves 6

THIS IS A GREAT DISH to make towards the end of summer when tomatoes are at their best. Saffron (or *krocous*, as it is known to Greeks) seems to have lost its place in Greek cooking over the years, but it is still highly regarded. Folklore has it that Zeus slept on a bed of saffron. I personally prefer using it in this dish.

Heat the olive oil in a large saucepan. Add the onion and garlic, and cook over a low heat for 10 minutes. Add the rice and stir for 1 minute. Now add the tomatoes, saffron, salt, pepper and stock. Bring to the boil and simmer for 15 minutes, stirring occasionally. Stir in the basil and place the prawns on top of the rice mixture. Cover the pan and cook for another 2–3 minutes. Remove from the heat and leave covered for another 5 minutes before serving.

PILAF OF SPINACH, DILL AND GRILLED SQUID

Spanakorizo me Kalamarakia Stin Skara

½ cup (125 mL/4 fl oz) extra
  virgin olive oil
300 g (10 oz) onions, finely
  chopped
2 cloves garlic, crushed
1⅓ cups (225 g/7 oz) short-grain
  rice, preferably arborio
½ teaspoon cumin seeds, dry-
  roasted and ground in spice mill
2 cups (500 mL/16 fl oz) light
  chicken stock
salt and freshly ground black
  pepper, to taste
1 kg (2 lb) young English spinach
  (spinach), trimmed, washed,
  dried and shredded
½ small bunch of fresh dill, finely
  chopped
½ small bunch of flat-leaf (Italian)
  parsley, finely chopped
grated rind and juice of 1 lemon
6-12 squid (calamari), cleaned and
  cut into 3 pieces (allow 1-2
  squid per person)
1 lemon (extra), cut into 6 wedges

Serves 6

SPANAKORIZO, AS THIS PILAF of spinach and dill is known, is a Greek national favourite. It is also a favourite with my friends. At the restaurant, we serve the pilaf with tender grilled squid pieces on top and a wedge of lemon. This delicious simplicity is what Greek cuisine is all about.

Heat the olive oil in a large saucepan, reserving 1 tablespoon for the squid. Add the onion and garlic and sauté until translucent. Now add the rice and cumin, and stir continuously for 2 minutes. Pour in the stock and add the salt and pepper. Reduce the heat to low, cover with a lid and simmer for 10 minutes.

Remove the lid and stir in the spinach, dill, parsley and lemon rind. Add a little water if the mixture seems too dry. The pilaf should be moist, with the rice grains separating easily. Replace the lid and cook for another 5–10 minutes, stirring occasionally. Add the lemon juice and remove the pan from the heat. Leave covered and set aside until the squid has been grilled.

Toss the squid pieces in the reserved oil and season with pepper. Place the squid pieces on a hot grill and cook on each side for 1 minute.

Divide the pilaf among 6 soup plates, pile the squid on top and garnish each serving with a wedge of lemon. Serve immediately.

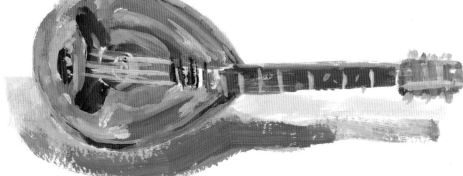

PILAF OF BRAISED QUAIL AND TOMATOES

Pilafi me Ortikia ke Tomates

100 mL (3 fl oz) virgin olive oil
*1 large brown (yellow) onion, finely
    chopped*
2 cloves garlic, crushed
6 quails, boned and halved
*1 teaspoon cumin seeds, dry-
    roasted and finely ground in a
    spice mill*
1 cup (250 mL/8 fl oz) red wine
*1 kg (2 lb) tomatoes, peeled, seeded
    and chopped*
1 cup (250 mL/8 fl oz) water
375 g (12 oz) arborio rice
*salt and freshly ground black
    pepper, to taste*
sugar, to taste

Serves 6

IN ALL THE YEARS that I have enjoyed my mother's cooking, nothing has been as comforting in winter as a bowl of this pilaf.

Pour the olive oil into a large saucepan. Sauté the onion and garlic in the oil over a medium heat until they are translucent. Add the quail or chicken to the onion mixture and cook for about 10 minutes, stirring constantly. Now add the cumin, wine, tomatoes and water. Slowly bring to the boil and simmer for 45 minutes.
   Add the rice and season with salt, pepper and sugar. Continue cooking for a further 15 minutes, stirring several times. Remove the pan from the heat and set aside, covered, for 10 minutes. Serve.

BRAISED CUTTLEFISH WITH SPINACH

Soupies me Spanakia

1.5 kg (3 lb) small cuttlefish,
  cleaned (keeping the ink sacs),
  or squid, cleaned
2 tablespoons tomato paste (pureé),
  if using squid only
½ cup (125 mL/4 fl oz) water
½ cup (125 mL/4 fl oz) dry white
  wine
100 mL (3 fl oz) extra virgin
  olive oil
2 Spanish (red) onions, peeled,
  halved and thinly sliced
½ tablespoon dried oregano
½ bunch of fresh flat-leaf (Italian)
  parsley, finely chopped
salt and freshly ground black
  pepper, to taste
1 kg (2 lb) young English spinach
  (spinach) leaves, trimmed,
  blanched and kept warm
1 lemon, cut into 6 wedges

Serves 6

CUTTLEFISH ARE A FAVOURITE food on the islands of Greece — especially this dish. This recipe is an adaptation of one I encountered throughout the island of Crete. You will often find cuttlefish in Asian markets, but squid can be used instead of cuttlefish if these are unavailable. If using squid, use tomato paste (pureé) in place of the cuttlefish ink.

If using cuttlefish, put the ink sacs and the water into a small bowl. Break the sacs with a fork to expel the ink. Strain through a fine sieve or strainer and add the wine to the ink mixture. Reserve liquid and discard ink sacs. Follow the same method for squid, with the tomato paste in place of the ink.

Add the olive oil to a large frying pan or skillet. Sauté the onion in the oil over a low heat, for about 10 minutes or until golden. Add the cuttlefish or squid and, stirring occasionally, cook for another 15 minutes.

Increase the heat and add the ink mixture and the oregano. Cook for a further 15 minutes. Stir in the parsley, salt and pepper.

Arrange the spinach leaves on 6 serving plates. Divide the cuttlefish (or squid) and its sauce among the plates, placing on top of the bed of spinach. Serve each portion with a wedge of lemon.

BAKED HALLOUMI TARTS WITH ASPARAGUS

Flaounes me Asparagia

PASTRY
¾ cup (185 mL/6 fl oz) virgin
*   olive oil*
2 eggs
¾ teaspoon aniseed, crushed
90 mL (3 fl oz) milk
5 cups (625 g/20 oz) bread (strong)
*   flour*
1 teaspoon baking powder
¾ teaspoon salt

FILLING
125 g (4 oz) halloumi *cheese*
125 g (4 oz) ricotta cheese
½ cup (125 mL/4 fl oz) thickened
*   (heavy, double) cream*
4 eggs
1 tablespoon finely chopped fresh
*   mint leaves*
12 fresh asparagus spears,
*   trimmed and halved lengthwise*

Makes 6 individual tarts

DURING EASTER CELEBRATIONS, the people of Cyprus bake lots of large savoury biscuits with a *halloumi* cheese filling, called *flaounes*. Late last year, I bought some *halloumi* and created this tart, using the flavour found in *flaounes* that I love so much.

Pastry: In a small bowl, lightly whisk the oil, eggs and aniseed together. Warm the milk in a small pan and stir into the egg mixture.

Place the dry ingredients into a food processor (or use an electric mixer with the dough hook attachment). With the motor running, pour in the egg mixture. When the dough gathers into a ball, remove and wrap in plastic wrap (cling film). Refrigerate for about 2 hours.

Filling: In a bowl, mix the *halloumi*, ricotta, cream, eggs and mint together well. Set aside.

To Bake the Tarts: Preheat the oven to 180°C (350°F/ gas mark 4). Roll out the pastry, cut into 6 circles and use to line 6 lightly greased 10 cm (4 in.) tart or pie pans. Fill the pastry shells with the cheese mixture and place 4 asparagus halves on top of each tart. Bake in the oven for 10 minutes, until just set. Remove and serve with a bitter green salad.

WARM EGGPLANT PIE WITH WALNUTS

Melitzanopitta me Karidia

3 medium eggplant (aubergines)
¼ cup (60 mL/2 fl oz) virgin olive oil
2 leeks (white parts only), thinly sliced
2 onions, finely chopped
2 cloves garlic, crushed
1 teaspoon cumin seeds, dry-roasted and ground in a spice mill
1 small bunch of fresh flat-leaf (Italian) parsley, stalks discarded and leaves finely chopped
250 g (8 oz) walnuts, lightly toasted and finely chopped
250 g (8 oz) kefalotyri or mild Parmesan cheese, grated
2 tablespoons semolina
3 eggs, lightly beaten
salt and freshly ground black pepper, to taste
12 sheets thick filo pastry
olive oil, as needed

Serves 8

I FIRST DISCOVERED this style of pie last year in Thessaloniki. The lady at the taverna told me that there are many variations of this recipe, but that I shouldn't ask for her version as it's been in her family for generations and she wouldn't part with it. She didn't part with it either! This is the version that I have created at my restaurant. It is delicious served with a side salad of rocket (arugula) and vine-ripened tomatoes simply dressed with a vinaigrette.

Hold the eggplants over a direct flame until their skins have blackened and blistered on all sides. When cool, remove the blackened skin and squeeze out the bitter juices and dark seeds. Finely chop the flesh and set aside.

Heat the olive oil in a pan and add the leeks, onions and garlic. Sauté until they are translucent.

Preheat the oven to 180°C (350°F/gas mark 4).

Mix the eggplant, onion mixture, cumin, parsley, walnuts, cheese, semolina, eggs, salt and pepper together in a large bowl.

Lightly oil a 23 cm (9 in.) square cake pan. Brush 4 sheets of filo with olive oil and cover the pan with the pastry. Leave the filo hanging over the edges of the pan. Pour in half the eggplant mixture. Oil another 4 sheets of filo and place one on top of the other. Cut into a circle slightly larger than the pan and place on top of the eggplant mixture. Pour in the remaining eggplant mixture. Brush the remaining 4 sheets of filo with olive oil and place on top of the pie. Gather and roll the top and bottom sheets of filo together and brush the top of the pie with more olive oil. Bake in the oven for 30–45 minutes. Leave to cool slightly and then serve.

ELENI'S MACARONI AND FETA PIE

Macaranopitta tis Elenis

CLASSIC FILO PASTRY

*4-5 cups (500-625 g/16-20 oz)
bread flour
1 teaspoon salt
¾ cup (185 mL/6 fl oz) chilled
water
4 tablespoons olive oil
a little olive oil (extra), as needed*

MACARONI AND FETA FILLING

*375 g (12 oz) tubular macaroni,
cooked for 8 minutes and
drained
500 g (1 lb) Greek sheep's milk or
other feta cheese (the best you
can afford)
8 eggs, lightly beaten
2½ cups (625 mL/20 fl oz) milk
150 mL (5 fl oz) single (light)
cream
salt, to taste
100 g (3 oz) butter, softened to
room temperature and cut into
cubes*

Serves 8

THIS PIE HAS BEEN a part of my mother's cooking for as long as I can recall. I don't think there has been a Christmas, birthday or nameday celebration where my mother hasn't made this pie. I love this pie, my family loves this pie, my mother loves making this pie. It originates from central Greece where my mother grew up — in Naupaktos, which is about an hour's drive from Delphi, a beautiful part of Greece.

Classic Filo Pastry: Sift 4 cups (500 g/16 oz) of the flour and the salt into a large bowl. Make a well in the centre of the flour and add the water and olive oil. Stir with a metal spoon until all the ingredients are combined. Turn out onto a lightly floured surface and knead until smooth and elastic, about 5-10 minutes. Add the remaining flour if needed. The dough should be pliable but not sticky.

Cover with plastic wrap (cling film) and set aside for 30 minutes. Divide into 4 equal balls. Keep each dough ball covered until you are ready to roll it out. Take one of the balls and place on a lightly floured surface. Roll out into a thin sheet, making a circle about 30 cm (12 in.) in diameter. Brush with a little extra olive oil. Repeat the process with another ball and place this one on top of the first sheet of pastry. Set aside. Repeat with the other 2 dough balls, so that you have two circles of double-layered dough when you are finished. Set aside.

Preheat the oven to 190°C (375°F/gas mark 5). Oil a 26 cm (10 in.) springform pan (or a pan with a removable base). Set aside.

Macaroni and Feta Filling: In a bowl, mix the macaroni, feta, eggs, milk, cream and salt (remember, the feta is quite salty).

To Assemble the Pie: Line the prepared pan with the first 2 filo sheets. Pour in the filling and spread around the pan, reserving ½ cup (125 mL/4 fl oz) of the mixture. Dot half the butter pieces over the filling. Cover with the 2 remaining sheets of filo. Gather and pinch the edges of the top and bottom sheets of filo. Pour the reserved liquid over the top and dot with the remaining butter. Bake in the oven for 45 minutes, until puffed and golden in colour.

When it has cooled slightly, carefully remove the pie from the pan. Serve hot or cold.

LAMB-FILLED MANTI WITH TZATZIKI AND ROAST TOMATO SALTSA

Manti me Tzatziki ke Tomata Saltsa

TZATZIKI

1 cup (250 mL/8 fl oz) yoghurt,
preferably sheep's or goat's milk
yoghurt
1 small cucumber, coarsely grated
with the skin on (place in a
clean cloth and wring to extract
excess juices after grating)
2 cloves garlic, crushed to a paste
1 tablespoon finely sliced fresh
mint leaves
1 tablespoon extra virgin olive oil

MANTI

150 g (5 oz) lean lamb mince
(ground lamb)
1 small onion, finely chopped
1 small bunch of fresh flat-leaf
(Italian) parsley, finely chopped
1 egg yolk
1 tablespoon olive oil
salt and freshly ground black
pepper, to taste
36 gow gee wrappers or won ton
skins (available from Asian
grocery stores), cut into circles
the width of the wrapper
1 egg white

MANTI ORIGINATED WITH the Asia Minor Greeks, prior to the Turkish invasion of Constantinople (now known as Istanbul). The stuffed pasta was cooked in a pot of tomato sauce and served with grated dry *myzithra* (ricotta). This dish has been forgotten by most cooks nowadays. I did, however, find a version of this dish made by an elderly woman from Crete. In her village they bake the *manti* and serve them simply with yoghurt.

Tzatziki: Combine all the ingredients for the tzatziki in a bowl. Cover with plastic wrap (cling film) and refrigerate until needed.

Manti: In a large bowl, combine the lamb, onion, parsley, egg yolk, olive oil, salt and pepper together well.

Place the wrappers or skins on greaseproof (wax) paper, leaving some space around each wrapper. Now place a spoonful of the filling mixture on one side of each wrapper and brush around the rim of each one with the egg white. Fold the empty side over and press firmly to seal the edges. You should have a semicircular parcel.

Repeat this process with all the wrappers and place in the refrigerator until needed.

ROAST TOMATO SALTSA
a little olive oil
2 kg (4 lb) very ripe tomatoes,
*   halved*
3 large brown (yellow) onions,
*   peeled and grated*
1 head of garlic, cloves separated
*   and peeled*
1 tablespoon Greek
*   (Mediterranean) oregano*
½ teaspoon sugar
salt and freshly ground black
*   pepper, to taste*
1 tablespoon tomato paste (purée)
100 mL (3 fl oz) white wine
150 mL (5 fl oz) light chicken
*   stock*

vegetable oil, for deep-frying
finely sliced fresh mint leaves, to
*   garnish*

Serves 6

Roast Tomato Saltsa: Preheat the oven to 180°C (350°F/gas mark 4). Grease a large baking dish with the olive oil. Place the tomatoes, onions and garlic in the dish. Sprinkle with the oregano, sugar, salt and pepper, and then add the tomato paste. Place in the oven until the tomatoes have softened and the onion and garlic are golden, about 40 minutes.

Remove from the oven, add the wine and stock, and return to the oven for a further 15 minutes.

Now remove from the oven and place the tomato mixture in an electric blender or food processor. Blend to a smooth purée then pass the sauce through a sieve. Adjust the seasoning if necessary. Keep the saltsa hot while cooking the *manti*. The oven is probably the best place to do this as you will also need to keep the *manti* warm until you are ready to serve them.

To Serve: Heat the oil to about 180°C (350°F) in a deep-fryer or large heavy saucepan. Place no more than 6 *manti* at a time into the hot oil and fry until golden in colour. Drain on paper towels or absorbent kitchen paper to remove excess oil. Place on a baking tray or sheet, and keep warm in the oven until all the *manti* are done. At the same time, heat 6 soup plates or deep-rimmed dinner plates.

When the *manti* are cooked, place several spoonfuls of Roast Tomato Saltsa onto each plate and place 6 *manti* in a circle on top of the saltsa. Put a spoonful of tzatziki on top of each *manti* and sprinkle with some finely sliced mint leaves. Serve immediately.

CYPRIOT-STYLE DUCK CAKES WITH YOGHURT TZATZIKI

Koupes me Papia ke Tzatziki

CRACKED WHEAT CASING

500 g (16 oz) fine cracked (bulghur) wheat
2 cups (500 mL/16 fl oz) hot water
1 teaspoon salt
1 tablespoon olive oil

MINCED DUCK

1 kg (2 lb) duck or chicken breasts, boned, skinned and the sinew removed
60 g (2 oz) pork back fat
1 small onion, finely chopped
1 clove garlic, finely chopped
½ small bunch of fresh parsley, finely chopped
1 teaspoon sea salt
1 teaspoon freshly ground black pepper
¼ teaspoon ground allspice
¼ cup (60 g/2 oz) pine nuts, toasted

KOUPES, AS THESE CAKES are known by Cypriots, are a market food found throughout the country. They resemble a stubby cigar, have a crisp outer coating made of cracked (bulghur) wheat and are filled with a spicy meat mixture, usually lamb.

I have taken this recipe a step further by making the filling with minced (ground) duck breast meat and serving the *koupes* on a green salad with a side dish of tangy tzatziki. They've become a favourite of my staff who are always insisting that I make a few more every time — 'just in case'.

Cracked Wheat Casing: Put the cracked wheat in a bowl, and pour the hot water over it. Add the salt and oil, and leave to stand for 1 hour. Place the mixture in an electric blender or food processor. Process until it forms a ball. Remove to a large bowl, cover with plastic wrap (cling film) and chill in the refrigerator.

Minced Duck: In a large bowl, combine the duck or chicken breasts, pork back fat, onion, garlic and spices together well. Cover and chill in the refrigerator for 1 hour. Pass the mixture through a mincer or meat grinder. When finely ground, stir the pine nuts into the mixture. Set aside.

TZATZIKI

*1 cup (250 mL/8 fl oz) sheep's
    milk yoghurt or Greek-style
    yoghurt*
*1 small cucumber, grated and
    squeezed dry*
2 cloves garlic, crushed
*4 large leaves of fresh mint, finely
    shredded*
1 tablespoon extra virgin olive oil
salt, to taste

vegetable oil, for frying
*assorted salad greens (such as
    rocket (arugula), chicory etc.),
    rinsed*

Makes 12

Tzatziki: Combine all the ingredients for the tzatziki and refrigerate for at least 1 hour before serving.

To Assemble the Dish: Take 1 tablespoon of the cracked wheat mixture and work into an egg shape with your hands. Carefully hollow this shape with your finger to form a thin casing (the thinner the casing, the better). Put a little of the duck mixture into the hollow and seal the open side. Repeat this process until you have 12 cakes.

In a deep, heavy frying pan or skillet, heat the oil to 180°C (350°F). Slip the cakes, a few at a time, into the hot oil. Fry until golden brown, about 5 minutes. Drain and serve on a salad of young green leaves with a dish of the tzatziki on the side to dip the cakes into.

RED PEPPER, FETA AND POTATO TERRINE WITH PINE NUT AND CURRANT DRESSING

Feta Forma me Piperies ke Patata

6 large red capsicum (bell peppers)
olive oil, as needed
2 waxy (boiling) potatoes (such as
*   desirée or pontiac)*
750 g (1½ lb) feta cheese,
*   crumbled*
100 mL (3 fl oz) plain yoghurt
¼ cup (60 mL/2 fl oz) olive oil

PINE NUT AND CURRANT
    DRESSING
¼ cup (60 mL/2 fl oz) red wine
*   vinegar*
1 tablespoon honey
salt and freshly ground black
*   pepper, to taste*
½ cup (125 mL/4 fl oz) extra
*   virgin olive oil*
⅔ cup (100 g/3 oz) currants
100 g (3 oz) pine nuts, lightly
*   roasted in oven*
1 clove garlic, crushed

Serves 12

THIS TERRINE IS great to serve as part of a buffet or for a special occasion for a large group of people. It looks quite dramatic when sliced and the dressing is similar to the sort made in the Peloponnese, generally around Corinth.

Preheat the oven to 230°C (450°F/gas mark 8).

Rub the capsicum with olive oil and roast in the oven until their skins have blackened. Remove, cover with a damp cloth and set aside for 1 hour. Now remove the blackened skin, cut each capsicum into quarters horizontally and discard the seeds. Pat dry between sheets of paper towels or absorbent kitchen paper, and set aside.

Meanwhile, boil the potatoes in their skins until tender.

Mix the feta with the yoghurt. Pureé in a food processor or food mill, then mix in the olive oil.

Line a triangular or square terrine dish of about 6 cups (1½ quarts/2½ imp. pts) capacity with plastic wrap (cling film). Cover the bottom of the dish with half the capsicum, and half the feta mixture. Peel the potatoes and slice thickly. Make a layer of these on top of the feta. Cover with the remaining feta and pat down firmly. Now cover with the remaining capsicum and seal the top with plastic wrap (cling film). Refrigerate overnight or for at least 6 hours.

Pine Nut and Currant Dressing: Whisk the vinegar, honey, salt and pepper in a small bowl. Slowly incorporate the oil, whisking all the time. Add the currants, pine nuts and garlic. Set aside for 1 hour to allow the flavours to develop.

To Serve: Unmould the terrine onto a serving plate. Serve with the Pine Nut and Currant Dressing.

SOUPS

MORE OFTEN THAN NOT, a soup will compose the entire meal in a Greek household, particularly during Lent, when a lentil soup or bean soup will be served with some fresh, crusty bread, an olive or two, and a glass of wine. Since ancient times, Greeks have believed in the fortifying powers of such soups. They have even been known to say that these hearty soups can develop mental and physical stamina.

Avgolemono, or egg and lemon soup, is by far the most common flavour in Greek soups, be it with chicken, fish or meat. The most unusual but flavourful example of this style of soup is *mageritsa* or lamb's innards soup. This soup is eaten after the midnight church service on Holy Saturday to break the lenten fast preceding Easter.

Fish soups are also a staple on Greek tables, especially on the islands. The most famous of these soups is *kakavia*, which is believed to have been introduced to the French by occupying Greeks of classical times, and is now known there as *bouillabaisse*.

LENTIL SOUP WITH SORREL AND TOMATO

Fakes me Lapeta ke Tomates

500 g (1 lb) large brown lentils
*½ cup (125 mL/4 fl oz) virgin
     olive oil*
2 large onions, finely chopped
8 cloves garlic, finely chopped
*1 small red chilli pepper, seeded
     and finely chopped*
2 bay leaves
*1 teaspoon dried Greek
     (Mediterranean) oregano*
*8 cups (2 L/3¼ imp. pts) light
     chicken stock or water*
*4 large, ripe tomatoes, peeled,
     seeded and chopped*
*2 bunches of fresh sorrel or
     1 bunch of English spinach
     (spinach), shredded*
*1 small bunch of fresh flat-leaf
     (Italian) parsley, finely chopped*
*1 teaspoon red wine vinegar (or
     2 teaspoons if using spinach)*
*salt and freshly ground black
     pepper, to taste*

Serves 8

LENTILS HAVE BEEN a vital part of Greek cuisine
since ancient times. Personally, I cannot remember
a winter whilst growing up when a lentil soup
wasn't served at our table. This soup has the acidity
of sorrel and tomato to balance the sweetness of the
lentils.

Soak the lentils overnight in plenty of cold water.
Heat the olive oil in a large saucepan, add the onion
and garlic, and cook over a low heat until golden in
colour (about 10 minutes). Drain and rinse the lentils
and add to the saucepan with the chilli, bay leaves,
oregano and stock or water. Bring to the boil, then
simmer for about 45 minutes. Just before serving,
add the tomato, sorrel or spinach, parsley, vinegar,
salt and pepper.

CHILLED OYSTER AND LEEK AVGOLEMONO SOUP

Kria Avgolemono Soupa me Stridia ke Prasa

100 mL (3 fl oz) virgin olive oil
1 kg (2 lb) leeks, white parts only,
    thinly sliced
1 onion, finely chopped
2 cloves garlic, crushed
2 stalks celery, sliced
1 cup (250 mL/8 fl oz) white wine
3 cups (750 mL/24 fl oz) light
    chicken stock
2 tablespoons ouzo
salt and freshly ground white
    pepper, to taste
6 egg yolks
3 egg whites
¼ cup (60 mL/2 fl oz) lemon juice
24 oysters, freshly shucked
½ bunch of fresh chives, finely
    chopped

Serves 6

THIS SOUP CAN BE served hot with the oysters poached in the soup. If serving chilled, it's better if the soup is made the day before it's needed.

Put the olive oil, leeks, onions, garlic and celery in a large saucepan. Cook over a low heat for 15 minutes, stirring every few minutes to prevent burning. Add the white wine to the saucepan and boil until the volume of the liquid is reduced by half, then add the stock, ouzo, salt and pepper. Simmer for 15 minutes. Now purée the soup in an electric blender or food processor in several batches. Return to a clean saucepan and keep hot while preparing the egg mixture.

Whisk the egg yolks and whites together in a bowl until thickened. Gradually add the lemon juice, continuing to whisk as you do so. Slowly pour 1 cup (250 mL/8 fl oz) of the soup into the egg mixture, whisking continuously to prevent the egg solidifying. Pour the egg mixture into the remaining soup and stir the soup over a low heat for 5 minutes. Do not let it come to the boil.

Place 4 oysters into each of 6 soup plates and ladle soup on top. Sprinkle the soup with chives and serve. If serving cold, chill the soup before adding the oysters.

VILLAGER'S BEAN SOUP WITH SPICY SAUSAGE

Fasolada me Loukanika

*375 g (12 oz) dried cannellini
    beans*
*½ cup (125 mL/4 fl oz) virgin
    olive oil*
*1 teaspoon cumin seeds, lightly
    roasted and crushed*
2 large onions, finely chopped
4 cloves garlic, finely chopped
3 large carrots, finely chopped
1 stalk celery, finely chopped
1 small celeriac, finely chopped
*6 cups (1.5 L/2½ imp. pts) chicken
    stock*
¼ teaspoon red pepper flakes
1 bay leaf
*3 sun-dried tomatoes, finely
    chopped*
*salt and freshly ground black
    pepper, to taste*
1 loukanika *or other sweet
    fresh pork sausage*
a little olive oil

Serves 6

BEAN SOUP HAS become synonymous with Greek cuisine. Some Greek cookbooks have dedicated whole chapters to it. I can even recall a time when I was much younger when a few of my aunties had come to visit our home whilst my mother was making her bean soup. All of them took great pride in wanting to share their 'secret' method or ingredients with her. Naturally she took no interest in theirs, preferring her own special recipe.

Soak the beans overnight, drain and rinse well.

Gently heat the olive oil over a low heat in a large saucepan. Add the cumin, onion, garlic, carrot, celery and celeriac. Sauté for about 15 minutes, until golden in colour. Now add the beans, stock, chilli, bay leaf and sun-dried tomatoes. Bring to the boil and simmer for 1 hour. Add salt and pepper.

While the soup is cooking, bring water to the boil for the sausage. Reduce the heat slightly and poach the sausage in simmering water for 5 minutes. Drain and cool. Heat a little olive oil in a frying pan or skillet. Slice the sausage and sauté in the oil until golden.

Ladle the soup into serving bowls and top each serve with several slices of the sausage. Serve immediately.

VEAL SHANK AVGOLEMONO SOUP WITH ORZO

Kreatosoupa me Manestra

1 veal shank
1 tablespoon olive oil
6 cups (1.5 L/2½ imp. pts) water
2 onions, sliced
1 carrot, sliced
1 stalk celery with leaves, sliced
3 cloves garlic, roughly chopped
1 teaspoon black peppercorns
1 teaspoon salt
3 whole allspice
1 strip of lemon rind
150 g (5 oz) orzo or other rice-
    shaped pasta
4 eggs, separated, at room
    temperature
pinch of salt
juice of 1 lemon

Serves 6

LAMB SHANKS MAY be used in this soup if veal shanks are difficult to find, simply increase the lemon flavour with the juice of one more lemon.

Put the veal shank and olive oil in a large saucepan. Brown the shank and drain off the fat.

Add the water, onion, carrot, celery, garlic, peppercorns, salt, allspice and lemon peel. Simmer the soup slowly for 2–3 hours, skimming the top occasionally.

Strain the soup through a fine sieve and a damp cloth. Shred the meat and reserve.

Return the soup to the saucepan and reheat. Stir in the orzo, cover the pan and simmer for about 20 minutes, until the orzo has cooked.

Beat the egg whites with the salt until soft peaks form. Add the egg yolks one at a time while still beating the whites, then slowly add the lemon juice.

Now slowly add a cup of the soup to the egg mixture, stirring all the time. Pour this mixture into the soup. Stir constantly for 2 minutes, until the soup thickens. Finally, stir in the reserved meat, heat through and serve.

ROAST TOMATO, LEEK AND CHICKPEA SOUP

Revitathia

ROAST TOMATO SAUCE

1 kg (2 lb) tomatoes, sliced in half

*1 large brown (yellow) onion,
    roughly chopped*

*1 head of garlic, cloves peeled and
    left whole*

2 tablespoons virgin olive oil

1 teaspoon dried oregano

1 tablespoon tomato paste (purée)

*salt, freshly ground black pepper
    and sugar, to taste*

SOUP

*½ cup (125 mL/4 fl oz) virgin
    olive oil*

*4 leeks, white parts only, cleaned
    and thinly sliced*

*250 g (8 oz) dried chickpeas
    (soaked overnight in cold water,
    drained and rinsed well)*

*6 cups (1.5 L/2½ imp. pts) light
    chicken stock or water*

1 bay leaf

ACCOMPANIMENT

*pita bread wedges, grilled or
    broiled*

Serves 6

THIS IS A GREAT soup served either hot or cold, with the flavour improving if it is made a day ahead.

Roast Tomato Sauce: Preheat the oven to 200°C (400°F/gas mark 6). Place all the ingredients for the sauce into a baking dish and mix well. Roast in the oven for 40 minutes. Pass through a food mill or blend in a food processor. Strain and set aside.

Soup: While the sauce is cooking, place the olive oil in a large, heavy saucepan. Add the leeks and cook over a low heat for 10 minutes. Stir in the chickpeas and cook for another 3 minutes. Now add the stock and bay leaf, and simmer the soup for 1 hour. Stir in the Roast Tomato Sauce, adjust the seasoning if necessary and simmer for another 30 minutes. Serve accompanied by the pita bread.

FISH AND SEAFOOD

AS THE SUN SETS on any of Greece's tiny island ports, fishermen are setting out for the night's fishing. By dawn, they will return with their bounty still smacking against the decks of their rickety fishing boats, ready to sell their catch at the local *agora* or share it among their families.

As the day begins, the fishermen are once again down by the ports mending and sorting their tangled nets, or slapping their catch of octopus against large rocks until it is ready to be grilled over hot coals for lunch.

Seafood has always been a major source of food for people living along the coastline and on the islands of Greece. As it is situated in the warmest part of the Mediterranean, Greece has always enjoyed an abundance of seafood in her emerald-blue waters.

Greeks have long enjoyed their seafood cooked simply and unadorned. In fact, methods of preparing and presenting fish have changed very little over the centuries.

Fish is always served whole with its head still intact, as to Greeks this is the tastiest and most nutritious part of a fish. Grilling and barbecuing are the most popular methods for cooking whole fish, simply brushed with olive oil, lemon juice and a few herbs. As with most meals, Greeks prefer fish dishes to be served tepid rather than hot. My mother says that this came about by means of necessity, so the cook could also cool down after cooking and enjoy her meal with the rest of the family.

HERBED TUNA STEAKS WITH ROAST TOMATOES AND DEEP-FRIED OKRA

Tonnos me Psites Tomates ke Bamies

ROAST TOMATOES

18 ripe egg (plum) tomatoes
extra virgin olive oil, as needed
salt, freshly ground black pepper
    and sugar, to taste
1 teaspoon dried Greek
    (Mediterranean) oregano

HERBED TUNA STEAKS

1 small onion, chopped
2 cloves garlic, peeled and chopped
½ bunch of fresh flat-leaf (Italian)
    parsley
1 tablespoon dried Greek
    (Mediterranean) oregano
1 teaspoon paprika
½ teaspoon salt
½ teaspoon freshly ground black
    pepper
finely grated rind and juice of
    1 lemon
⅓ cup (90 mL/3 fl oz) extra virgin
    olive oil
6 tuna steaks, each 225 g (7 oz)

THE HERB PASTE in this dish is traditionally made as a marinade and used to flavour a whole baked fish, which would be served with deep-fried potato wedges. This is a more refined version, but both are equally delicious.

Roast Tomatoes: Preheat the oven to 160°C (325°F/gas mark 3). Place the tomatoes in a baking dish and coat with the olive oil. Season with the salt, pepper, sugar and oregano. Bake for 30 minutes. Set aside and keep warm.

Herbed Tuna Steaks: Preheat the oven to 200°C (400°F/gas mark 6). Place the onion, garlic, parsley, oregano, paprika, salt, pepper and lemon rind and juice in an electric blender or food processor. Process to combine. With the motor still running, slowly pour in the olive oil until it forms a thick paste.

Cut 6 sheets of aluminium foil to 40 cm (16 in.) in length, and fold in half. Place a spoonful of herb paste in the centre of each sheet of foil and place a tuna steak on top. Coat the tuna with another spoonful of paste. Wrap the tuna in the foil and bake in the oven for 10 minutes. Meanwhile, prepare the okra.

DEEP-FRIED OKRA
500 g (1 lb) okra
salt, as needed
vinegar, as needed
vegetable oil, for deep-frying

GARNISH
1 lemon, cut into 6 wedges

Serves 6

Deep-fried Okra: Trim the tops from the okra. Sprinkle liberally with salt and vinegar. Set aside for at least 1 hour to allow the juices from the okra to disgorge. Rinse and drain the okra. Deep-fry in vegetable oil for 6–7 minutes, until golden and crisp. Drain on paper towels or absorbent kitchen paper.

To Serve: Have 6 warmed dinner plates ready. Unwrap the tuna parcels and place one on each plate with its cooking juices. Surround with Roast Tomatoes and the okra. Serve immediately with a wedge of lemon as garnish.

SARDINE FILLETS IN VINE LEAVES WITH ROSEMARY VINEGAR SAUCE

Sardeles se Ambelofila ke Saltsa Marinata

MARINADE
¼ cup (60 mL/2 fl oz) virgin
   olive oil
¼ cup (60 mL/2 fl oz) lemon juice
1 teaspoon chopped fresh rosemary
   needles
salt and freshly ground black
   pepper, to taste

SARDINE FILLETS
1 kg (2 lb) sardines, cleaned, boned
   and left whole (ask your
   fishmonger)
2 heads of garlic, slowly roasted
   and the cloves mashed with a
   fork
fresh vine (grape) leaves, blanched
   and dried, or preserved vine
   leaves, rinsed in cold water and
   dried

ROSEMARY VINEGAR SAUCE
juices reserved from the baked
   sardines
100 mL (3 fl oz) extra virgin
   olive oil
1 clove garlic, finely chopped
100 mL (3 fl oz) red wine vinegar
¼ cup (60 mL/2 fl oz) water
1 tablespoon fresh rosemary
   needles
4 bay leaves
salt and freshly ground black
   pepper, to taste

ACCOMPANIMENT
deep-fried potatoes (see page 67)

FRESH SARDINES ARE cooked everywhere in Greece, usually fried and served with wedges of lemon or baked in a spicy tomato sauce.

This recipe is an adaptation of one from Macedonia, where almost any small fish is used to make the dish. It is delicious with the sauce poured over the top of the sardines and accompanied by deep-fried potatoes or French fries.

Marinade: Combine all the ingredients for the marinade.

Sardine Fillets: Place the sardine fillets in a large bowl and cover with the marinade. Leave to marinate for 30 minutes.

Preheat the oven to 200°C (400°F/gas mark 6).

Remove the sardines from the marinade. Reserve the marinade. Place a little mashed garlic in the cavity of each sardine. Wrap each sardine in a vine leaf. Layer sardines in a greased baking dish and pour the reserved marinade over them. Bake in the oven for 20 minutes. Keep warm while preparing the Rosemary Vinegar Sauce.

Rosemary Vinegar Sauce: Heat the reserved juices from the sardines, olive oil and garlic in a small saucepan. Whisk the vinegar, water, rosemary and bay leaves together. Add to the pan and simmer for 5 minutes. Adjust the seasoning with salt and pepper, and pour the sauce over the fish.

Serve immediately with the deep-fried potatoes.

PLAKI OF SNAPPER WITH SPRING VEGETABLES

Psari Plaki me Horta

6 large snapper fillets, cleaned

juice of 1 lemon

2 tablespoons olive oil

½ teaspoon salt

3 tomatoes, peeled, seeded and
    chopped

1 onion, finely chopped

2 stalks celery, finely chopped

1 teaspoon chopped fresh rosemary
    needles

¼ cup (60 mL/2 fl oz) olive oil
    (extra)

225 mL (7 fl oz) white wine

1 bunch of baby carrots, trimmed
    and blanched in boiling water
    for 1 minute, then refreshed in
    cold water

1 bunch of fresh asparagus,
    trimmed and blanched as above

12 small zucchini (courgettes) with
    flowers attached, blanched as
    above, then cut lengthwise

2 large waxy (boiling) potatoes,
    parboiled, peeled and sliced

Serves 6

PLAKI IS A STYLE OF cooking in which the fish is covered with vegetables and baked in a lemon and tomato sauce.

Place the snapper fillets in a large bowl. Combine the lemon juice, olive oil, salt, tomatoes, onion, celery and rosemary in another bowl. Pour over the fish, cover and refrigerate for 1-2 hours.

Preheat the oven to 220°C (425°F/gas mark 7). Remove the snapper fillets from the marinade. Set aside.

Pour the marinade into a saucepan. Add the extra olive oil and cook over a moderate heat for 5 minutes. Add the wine and simmer for another 5 minutes. Set aside to cool.

Place the snapper fillets in 6 individual oiled baking dishes or 1 large dish. Toss the carrot, asparagus, zucchini and potatoes together. Use this mixture to cover the snapper fillets. Pour the wine sauce over the top. Bake in the oven for 10 minutes and serve immediately with lots of fresh, crusty bread.

BRAISED SQUID STUFFED WITH PRAWNS, RICE AND GARLIC

Kalamaria me Garides, Risi ke Skordo

*1/3 cup (90 mL/3 fl oz) virgin
   olive oil*
1 onion, finely chopped
4 cloves garlic, finely chopped
1 cup (150 g/5 oz) long-grain rice
2 tablespoons pine nuts
100 mL (3 fl oz) white wine
1 cup (250 mL/8 fl oz) water
2 tablespoons currants
*salt and freshly ground black
   pepper, to taste*
*handful of fresh flat-leaf (Italian)
   parsley, finely chopped*
*225 g (7 oz) green (uncooked)
   prawns (shrimp), peeled and
   chopped*
1.5 kg (3 lb) squid tubes, cleaned
*1 cup (250 mL/8 fl oz) Roast
   Tomato Saltsa (see page 35)*
virgin olive oil, as needed
*2 bunches of English spinach
   (spinach) or wild greens (such as
   amaranth), trimmed and
   blanched*

Serves 6

IF SERVED SIMPLY and not overcooked, squid makes a delicious focus for any meal. This dish can also be used as a *mezes*, simply slice the squid thinly and serve without the greens.

Heat the olive oil in a saucepan over a moderate heat. Add the onion and garlic, and sauté until translucent. Add the rice and pine nuts. Sauté for another minute, stirring continuously. Now add the wine and allow it to be absorbed before adding the water. Lastly add the currants and season with salt and pepper. Reduce the heat to low and simmer. When the water has been absorbed, remove from the heat and cool.

Preheat the oven to 180°C (350°F/gas mark 4).

When the rice mixture is cool, stir through the parsley and prawns. Fill each squid tube with this filling. Close the ends with toothpicks (cocktail sticks).

Put the Roast Tomato Saltsa and some olive oil into a baking dish and place the squid in the sauce. Bake in the oven for 30 minutes.

Make a bed of spinach or greens on each serving plate. Place a serving of squid with some of its sauce on each plate. Serve immediately.

BAKED OCEAN TROUT WITH TOMATO CUMIN SALTSA

Pestrofa Psiti me Saltsa Tomatas ke Kimino

TOMATO CUMIN SALTSA
¼ cup (60 mL/2 fl oz) virgin
*   olive oil*
1 large brown (yellow) onion, finely
*   chopped*
1 leek, white part only, finely sliced
1 clove garlic, finely chopped
1.5 kg (3 lb) ripe tomatoes, peeled,
*   seeded and finely chopped*
1 bay leaf
1 tablespoon cumin seeds, dry-
*   roasted and ground in a spice*
*   mill*
salt, freshly ground black pepper
*   and sugar, to taste*

OCEAN TROUT
6 ocean trout or salmon fillets,
*   each 185 g (6 oz)*
virgin olive oil, as needed
salt and freshly ground black
*   pepper, to taste*
1 small bunch of English spinach
*   (spinach), leaves blanched and*
*   dried*
300 g (10 oz) kataifi *pastry*

Serves 6

KATAIFI IS FILO PASTRY that is shredded finely and resembles vermicelli. If you cannot find *kataifi*, use filo pastry and shred with a knife. It is mainly used for making desserts. At Cosmos, we use it as a pastry casing for our baked ocean trout. The trout remains quite moist and tender inside the wispy, crisp *kataifi* pastry.

Tomato Cumin Saltsa: Heat the olive oil in a saucepan over a moderate heat. Add the onion, leek and garlic. Sauté until they are translucent. Add the tomatoes, bay leaf, cumin, salt, pepper and sugar. Simmer over a low heat for 30–40 minutes. Keep warm and remove the bay leaf before serving.

Ocean Trout: Preheat the oven to 200°C (400°F/ gas mark 6). Brush each fillet with olive oil and season with salt and pepper. Wrap each fillet in some blanched spinach leaves.

Spread out the pastry and divide into 6 pieces. Wrap each fillet tightly in the pastry and brush liberally with olive oil. Place the wrapped fillets on a greased baking tray (sheet) and bake for 10–12 minutes. Serve hot with the Tomato Cumin Saltsa.

STEAMED GROUPER ON A CHICKPEA CAKE WITH TAHINI SALTSA AND BABY BEANS

Rophos me Revithokeftedes, Tahinosalata ke Fasoulia

CHICKPEA CAKES

125 g (4 oz) dried chickpeas
½ teaspoon bicarbonate of soda
(baking soda)
1 onion, finely chopped
2 cloves garlic, finely chopped
1 teaspoon cumin seeds
2 eggs, lightly beaten
¼ cup (60 mL/2 fl oz) olive oil
1 teaspoon red wine vinegar
handful of fresh flat-leaf (Italian)
parsley, finely chopped
1 tablespoon finely chopped fresh
dill
60 g (2 oz) kefalotyri *or pecorino*
cheese, grated
salt and freshly ground black
pepper, to taste
light olive oil, for frying

TAHINI SALTSA

150 mL (5 fl oz) tahini paste
2 cloves garlic, finely chopped
½ cup (125 mL/4 fl oz) cold water
juice of 2 small lemons
salt, to taste
¼ cup (60 mL/2 fl oz) extra virgin
olive oil

STEAMED GROUPER

6 grouper fillets, each 185 g (6 oz)
500 g (2 lb) baby green (French or
string) beans, stem end removed
extra virgin olive oil, as needed

Serves 6

CHICKPEA CAKES ARE a speciality of the Dodecanese Islands, where they are served cold with a bowl of tahini saltsa for dipping. I have taken this dish one step further and serve it as a main course topped with steamed fillets of grouper and baby green beans.

Chickpea Cakes: Soak the chickpeas overnight in plenty of cold water and the bicarbonate of soda. Drain and rinse well.

Place the chickpeas, onion, garlic and cumin seeds in an electric blender or food processor. Process to a coarse meal. Mix the eggs, olive oil, vinegar, parsley, dill, cheese, salt and pepper together in a large bowl. Stir in the chickpea mixture until well incorporated.

Cover the bottom of a large frying pan or skillet with the light olive oil and heat. When hot, drop large spoonfuls of the batter in the oil, making 6 large cakes. Fry until browned on both sides. Drain on paper towels or absorbent kitchen paper, and keep warm.

Tahini Saltsa: Process the tahini, garlic, water, lemon juice and salt in an electric blender or food processor until smooth. With the motor running, slowly pour in the oil and process until thick. Cover and chill.

Steamed Grouper: Cook the grouper fillets in a large steamer for 6-7 minutes. Cook the baby green beans for 2 minutes in a large saucepan. Drain and toss with a little olive oil.

To Serve: Place a chickpea cake on each of 6 pre-heated serving plates. Cover with the saltsa, then place a grouper fillet on top. Finally top with the baby beans and some of their dressing. Serve immediately.

TUNA WITH CELERIAC SKORDALIA AND BROAD BEANS

Tonnos me Skordalia Apo Selinorisa ke Koukia

CELERIAC SKORDALIA
500 g (1 lb) celeriac (celery root),
   peeled and diced
4 cloves garlic, finely chopped
juice of 1½ lemons
salt and freshly ground white
   pepper, to taste
225 mL (7 fl oz) virgin olive oil
100 mL (3 fl oz) milk

TUNA
6 tuna steaks, each 225 g (7 oz)
virgin olive oil, as needed
salt and freshly ground black
   pepper, to taste

BROAD BEANS
1 kg (2 lb) fresh young broad (fava)
   beans, double peeled and
   blanched, or fresh peas
½ cup (125 mL/4 fl oz) virgin
   olive oil (extra)
salt, to taste

1 lemon, cut into 6 wedges

Serves 6

BROAD (FAVA) BEANS ARE one of my favourite spring vegetables, but they must be double peeled and very fresh. The beans work well in this dish of grilled tuna which is served with celeriac and garlic purée.

Celeriac Skordalia: Boil the celeriac in a large saucepan for 30 minutes, until tender. Drain. Process the celeriac, garlic, lemon juice, salt and pepper in an electric blender or food processor. With the motor running, slowly pour in the oil, then pour in the milk. Keep the skordalia warm until needed.

Tuna: Preheat the grill or broiler. Brush the tuna with olive oil and season with salt and pepper. Cook for 2 minutes on both sides. Keep warm.

Broad Beans: Place the broad beans (or peas), extra olive oil and salt in a small saucepan and warm through gently.

To Serve: Spoon some Celeriac Skordalia onto each serving plate, then top with grilled tuna. Place the broad beans and their sauce over the top of the tuna. Serve immediately, each plate garnished with a lemon wedge.

ROAST KING PRAWNS WITH SPINACH, HERBS AND FETA

Garides Psites me Spanaki, Skordo ke Feta

*2 bunches of English spinach
    (spinach), trimmed and
    blanched*
*1.5 kg (3 lb) green (uncooked) king
    prawns (jumbo shrimp), peeled,
    deveined and tails left intact*
*3 ripe tomatoes, peeled, seeded and
    quartered*
*2 heads of garlic, peeled and
    poached in fish or chicken stock
    for 10 minutes*
*100 mL (3 fl oz) extra virgin
    olive oil*
juice of 2 lemons
*1½ small bunches of fresh dill,
    finely chopped*
*½ small bunch of fresh oregano,
    finely chopped*
freshly ground black pepper, to taste
*300 g (10 oz) goat's milk or other
    feta cheese, cut into 1 cm
    (½ in.) cubes*

Serves 6

PRAWNS (SHRIMP) COOKED WITH feta make their appearance on the menu of many tavernas throughout Greece. We serve this version as a main course, and it needs nothing more than some good crusty bread to mop up all the delicious juices.

Preheat the oven to 220°C (425°F/gas mark 7).

Oil 6 individual baking dishes or 1 large baking dish. Cover the bottom of the dishes or dish with spinach. Add the prawns, tomato pieces and garlic.

Whisk the olive oil and lemon juice together in a small bowl. Pour over the prawns. Mix the herbs together and sprinkle over the prawns. Season with pepper. Bake in the oven for 10 minutes. Top with the feta cheese and serve immediately.

RED MULLET WITH LEEK FRITTERS ON A SAVORO SAUCE

Barbounia me Prassopittes ke Saltsa Savoro

SAVORO SAUCE
virgin olive oil, as needed
1 large brown (yellow) onion, finely
*   chopped*
1 clove garlic, finely chopped
1 kg (2 lb) ripe tomatoes, peeled,
*   seeded and chopped*
30 mL (1 fl oz) red wine vinegar
1 tablespoon honey
90 mL (3 fl oz) fish stock
pinch of saffron threads
½ cinnamon stick
2 bay leaves
1 tablespoon finely chopped thyme
salt and freshly ground black
*   pepper, to taste*
⅓ cup (60 g/2 oz) currants

BARBOUNIA, OR RED MULLET, is the most highly prized fish in Greece and many other parts of the Mediterranean. History notes that the Ancient Greeks regarded it as sacred and food fit only for the gods. Savoro sauce is commonly partnered with this fish in many homes and tavernas throughout Greece. The *barbounia* are almost always served whole and cold, marinated in the sauce. At Cosmos, we serve the fillets hot, on top of creamy leek fritters and savoro sauce.

Savoro Sauce: Heat the olive oil in a saucepan over a moderate heat. Add the onion and garlic, and sauté until they are translucent. Now add the tomatoes, vinegar, honey, stock, saffron, herbs and spices. Simmer for 5 minutes. Lastly add the currants and simmer for 25 minutes. Keep warm.

LEEK FRITTERS

*2 leeks, white parts only, thinly
    sliced*

1 tablespoon olive oil

*150 g (5 oz) goat's milk or other
    feta cheese, grated*

*½ small bunch of fresh flat-leaf
    (Italian) parsley, finely chopped*

*½ bunch of fresh oregano, finely
    chopped*

*2 eggs plus 1 extra egg yolk,
    separated*

*½ cup (60 g/2 oz) plain (all-
    purpose) flour, sifted*

freshly ground black pepper, to taste

olive oil, for frying

RED MULLET

*9 large red mullet, filleted (ask
    your fishmonger)*

flour, to coat fish

olive oil, for frying

red wine vinegar, to deglaze pan

Serves 6

Leek Fritters: Cook the leeks in the olive oil over a
moderate heat until they are golden in colour. Cool.

Stir the leeks, feta, herbs, egg yolks and flour
together in a large bowl. Season with pepper. Whisk
the egg whites until stiff and fold through the
mixture.

Cover the bottom of a frying pan or skillet with
olive oil and heat. When hot, fry tablespoonfuls of the
batter in the oil until golden on both sides. Drain on
paper towels (absorbent kitchen paper) and keep
warm.

Red Mullet: Lightly coast the fish in flour. Fry for
1-2 minutes on both sides in olive oil.

To Serve: Place some Savoro Sauce on each serving
plate, and top with 2 or 3 Leek Fritters. Divide the
red mullet fillets among the serving plates, placing
them on top of the fritters.

Drain the oil from the frying pan or skillet used to
cook the fish. Add some red wine vinegar to the pan
to deglaze. Pour over the fillets and serve
immediately.

OCEAN TROUT WITH SCALLOP MOUSSE WRAPPED IN VINE LEAVES ON AN AVGOLEMONO SAUCE

Pestrofa Thalassini me Ktenia se Ambelofila me Avgolemono

1 ocean trout or salmon, about
   1 kg (2 lb), skinned and boned
185 g (6 oz) scallop meat, without
   roe
2 small egg whites
1 teaspoon salt
a few drops of Tabasco sauce
¼ cup (60 mL/2 fl oz) thickened
   (heavy, double) cream
12 large preserved vine (grape)
   leaves, drained, washed and
   drained again

AVGOLEMONO SAUCE
225 mL (7 fl oz) fish or chicken
   stock
¼ cup (60 mL/2 fl oz) white wine
4 large egg yolks
⅓ cup (90 mL/3 fl oz) lemon juice
1 tablespoon chopped fresh dill
salt, to taste

ACCOMPANIMENT
deep-fried potatoes (see page 67)

Serves 6

VINE (GRAPE) LEAVES ARE commonly used in Greek cooking and have become synonymous with the 'true flavour' of the Aegean. *Dolmathes* (vine-stuffed parcels) served in *avgolemono* soup are one of the most popular examples of this. In Greece, only the tender young leaves are used, and only a few of these are taken from the top third of each vine during spring and early summer.

Check the trout or salmon for any small bones and remove them with a pair of tweezers. Cut the fish in half lengthwise. Refrigerate.

Chill the bowl and blade of a food processor in the freezer for 1 hour. Remove and process the scallops, egg whites, salt and Tabasco sauce until smooth. Pour into a bowl and fold the cream through. Cover and refrigerate.

Spread a sheet of plastic wrap (cling film) about 60 cm (24 in.) in length across the top of a flat work surface. Place 8 of the vine leaves on top of the wrap, in 2 rows of 4 leaves, making sure the leaves slightly overlap each other. Place one of the trout or salmon fillets lengthwise in the centre of one of the rows of leaves. Spread the scallop mousse onto the fillet and cover with the second fillet. Place the remaining vine leaves on top of this fillet and wrap the vine leaves tightly around the fish with the plastic wrap. Freeze for 2 hours until firm.

Bring a large steamer of water to the boil. Remove the fish from the freezer, take out of the plastic wrap, and cut into 6 portions. Place in the steamer and cook for 8–10 minutes.

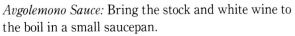

Avgolemono Sauce: Bring the stock and white wine to the boil in a small saucepan.

Whisk the egg yolks until they are pale and creamy. Slowly add the lemon juice, whisking all the time. Whisk for 1 minute longer. Slowly pour in the boiling stock, whisking continuously. Pour back into the saucepan and simmer for 3 minutes, stirring continuously. Add the dill and salt.

To Serve: Place a portion of fish on each of 6 warmed dinner plates. Pour some Avgolemono Sauce around each serving and add some deep-fried potato wedges to each plate. Serve immediately.

MUSSEL PILAF
Pilafi me Mithia

*42-48 mussels or clams, scrubbed,
    with the 'beards' removed*
*2-2½ cups (500-625 mL/
    16-20 fl oz) chicken stock or
    fish stock or water*
*large pinch of saffron threads, dry-
    roasted in a pan for 1 minute*
150 mL (5 fl oz) virgin olive oil
*2 brown (yellow) onions, finely
    chopped*
2 cups (375 g/12 oz) arborio rice
*salt and freshly ground black
    pepper, to taste*
small handful of fresh dill, chopped
*100 g (3 oz) pine nuts, lightly
    toasted*
⅓ cup (60 g/2 oz) currants
1 lemon, cut into 6 wedges

Serves 6

THIS *PILAFI* WORKS WELL with most shellfish. It also makes a substantial vegetarian meal if the shellfish is replaced with cauliflower or broccoli florets.

Place the mussels or clams in a large saucepan, cover and cook over a high heat for about 2 minutes, until all the mussels open, shaking the pan occasionally. Strain the liquid from the mussels, through a cloth-lined sieve, into a bowl. Add enough of the stock to this liquid to make it 3 cups (750 mL/24 fl oz). Now add the saffron to the liquid and set aside.

Remove the mussels from their shells and place in a bowl. Cover and set aside.

Heat the olive oil in a large saucepan over a moderate heat. Add the onion and sauté until it is golden in colour. Add the rice and, stirring continuously, cook for 1-2 minutes. Now add the stock mixture and bring to the boil. Simmer, uncovered and without stirring, until all the liquid has been absorbed, about 10-12 minutes. Turn off the heat.

Add the mussels, salt, pepper, dill, pine nuts and currants. Cover the saucepan with a clean cloth and lid, and set aside for 15 minutes. Stir the *pilafi* and serve immediately, each serving garnished with a lemon wedge.

OCTOPUS STEW WITH HILOPITTES AND PARSLEY SALATA

Oktapodi Brasto me Hilopittes ke Mantanosalata

½ cup (125 mL/4 fl oz) virgin
   olive oil
2 large onions, finely chopped
1.5 kg (3 lb) medium-sized octopus,
   with the head sacs removed,
   washed and cut into pieces
1 kg (2 lb) ripe tomatoes, peeled,
   seeded and chopped
1 clove garlic, finely chopped
225 mL (7 fl oz) red wine
1 bay leaf, torn
1 stick cinnamon
1 small red chilli pepper, seeded
   and chopped
grated rind of ½ orange
sugar, salt and freshly ground
   black pepper, to taste
500 g (1 lb) hilopittes (available
   in Greek delicatessens) or other
   small, square-shaped pasta

PARSLEY SALATA

1 cup (60 g/2 oz) fresh
   breadcrumbs
1 small onion, finely chopped
6 cloves garlic, peeled and blanched
2 bunches of fresh flat-leaf (Italian)
   parsley, trimmed of tough
   stalks, washed and dried
1 egg yolk
juice of 1 lemon
100 mL (3 fl oz) virgin olive oil
salt and freshly ground black
   pepper, to taste

Serves 6

THIS RICH, FLAVOURFUL STEW is the perfect dish to serve on a cold, wintry night. *Hilopittes* is a small, rectangular-shaped pasta made with equal portions of eggs and goat's milk in the dough.

Octopus Stew: Heat the olive oil in a large saucepan over a moderate heat. Add the onion and sauté until it is translucent. Reduce the heat to low and add the octopus pieces. Cook, stirring occasionally, until the octopus turn a rich, pink colour (about 15 minutes).

Add the tomatoes, garlic, wine, bay leaf, cinnamon and chilli pepper. Bring the stew to the boil, reduce the heat and simmer, covered, for 1½ hours, until the octopus is tender. Add the orange rind, sugar, salt and pepper, and simmer for a further 30 minutes.

Parsley Salata: Place the breadcrumbs, onion, garlic and parsley in an electric blender or food processor. Process for 30 seconds. With the motor still running, add the egg yolk and lemon juice, and then slowly add the olive oil. Season with salt and pepper. Pour into a container, cover and refrigerate until needed.

To Serve: Bring a large saucepan of salted water to the boil. Add the pasta and cook until tender. Drain.

Divide the pasta among 6 large soup plates or wide-rimmed dinner plates. Top with some octopus and its sauce, and a spoonful of Parsley Salata. Serve immediately.

ATLANTIC SALMON WITH PINK TARAMASALATA AND ASPARAGUS

Psari me Taramasalata ke Asparagia

PINK TARAMASALATA
½ white onion, finely chopped
1 clove garlic, finely chopped
3 slices white bread, crusts
   removed and soaked in ¼ cup
   (60 mL/2 fl oz) water
juice of 1 large lemon
100 g (3 oz) tarama
150 mL (5 fl oz) extra virgin
   olive oil
lemon juice (extra), to taste

AVGOLEMONO SAUCE
150 mL (5 fl oz) fish, shellfish or
   light chicken stock
150 mL (5 fl oz) dry white wine
5 egg yolks
juice of 1 lemon
salt and freshly ground black
   pepper, to taste

ATLANTIC SALMON FILLETS
6 Atlantic salmon fillets, each
   185 g (6 oz)
virgin olive oil, as needed
salt and freshly ground black
   pepper, to taste
750 g (1½ lb) small new potatoes,
   boiled until tender and halved
750 g (1½ lb) fresh asparagus,
   steamed until tender and
   refreshed in cold water
handful of fresh basil leaves,
   shredded

Serves 6

TARAMASALATA IS EASILY the most widely consumed dish in Greece during Lent, when no meat nor dairy products can be eaten. I have been told that even the Ancient Greeks were fond of this fish spread. In this dish, I accompany it with some fantastic spring produce to create a light but flavour-packed meal.

Pink Taramasalata: Process the onion, garlic, bread and lemon juice in an electric blender or food processor until smooth. Add the tarama and process for 1 minute. With the motor still running, slowly pour in the oil. Add extra lemon juice if needed. Cover and refrigerate.

Avgolemono Sauce: Bring the stock and wine to the boil in a saucepan. In a bowl, whisk the egg yolks with the lemon juice until creamy. Slowly pour into the stock mixture, whisking continuously. Season with salt and pepper. Simmer for 1 minute. Keep the sauce warm until needed.

Atlantic Salmon Fillets: Preheat the oven to 220°C (425°F/gas mark 7).
   Heat a frying pan or skillet until very hot. Brush the salmon fillets with olive oil and season with salt and pepper.
   Place in the pan and cook for 1 minute. Turn the fillets over and cook in the oven for 4 minutes on the other side.
   Meanwhile, add the potatoes, asparagus and basil to the Avgolemono Sauce and gently reheat.
   Divide the vegetables among 6 serving plates. Place a salmon fillet on top of each serving. Top each fillet with a spoonful of Pink Taramasalata and serve immediately.

GRILLED SWORDFISH WITH DEEP-FRIED POTATOES, OLIVES, LEMONS AND PARSLEY

Xifias Sti Skara me Patates, Elies, Lemonia ke Mantano

6 swordfish steaks

150 mL (5 fl oz) extra virgin olive oil

juice of 1 lemon

1 tablespoon finely chopped fresh thyme

1 teaspoon finely chopped fresh marjoram

2 bay leaves, crumbled

salt and freshly ground black pepper, to taste

vegetable oil, to deep-fry the potatoes

500 g (1 lb) small new potatoes, parboiled for 10 minutes and refreshed in cold water

3 lemons, peeled of all skin and pith, and cut into segments, with the membrane between segments removed

100 g (3 oz) kalamata olives, pitted and halved

handful of fresh flat-leaf (Italian) parsley, leaves roughly chopped

1 tablespoon preserved lemon (see page 111), finely chopped

100 mL (3 fl oz) extra virgin olive oil (extra)

Serves 6

SWORDFISH IS HIGHLY PRIZED throughout the Greek islands. In Sicily in the eighteenth century, a traveller wrote about the fishermen there who spoke Greek as a charm to lure the swordfish to their boats, for they believed if they spoke even a word of Italian, the swordfish would flee, never to return.

Place the swordfish steaks into a large, shallow dish. Whisk the oil, lemon juice, thyme, marjoram, bay leaf, salt and pepper in a small bowl. Pour over the fish and marinate for 30 minutes.

Preheat a grill plate or barbecue. Grill the swordfish for about 4 minutes on each side, keeping the centre moist. Meanwhile, preheat the vegetable oil to 180°C (350°F) in a deep-fryer. Fry the potatoes until they are golden in colour. Drain.

Mix the lemon segments, olives, parsley, preserved lemon and extra olive oil in a small bowl.

Place a grilled swordfish steak on each of 6 warmed dinner plates. Surround with deep-fried potatoes and top with some lemon mixture. Serve immediately.

TOMATO-ROASTED OCTOPUS WITH SPINACH AND ROAST RED PEPPERS

Oktapodi Psito me Spanakia ke Piperies Psites

TOMATO MARINADE
3 sun-dried tomatoes in olive oil,
   sliced
3 tablespoons reserved oil from
   sun-dried tomatoes or olive oil
4 cloves garlic, finely chopped
1/3 cup (100 mL/3 fl oz) tomato
   paste (purée)
2 tablespoons red wine vinegar
100 mL (3 fl oz) red wine
1 tablespoon sugar
1 tablespoon dried Greek
   (Mediterranean) oregano
freshly ground black pepper, to taste

1.5 kg (3 lb) baby octopus, cleaned
2 bunches of English spinach
   (spinach), trimmed and washed
2 red capsicum (bell peppers),
   roasted, peeled and cut into
   thick slices (see page 38)

Serves 6

MY FIRST MEMORY OF octopus is of an elderly fisherman beating them against a large stone by the water's edge near Naupatkos in central Greece.

Combine all the marinade ingredients together well in a large bowl. Add the octopus, cover and refrigerate for 4–6 hours.
   Preheat the oven to 220°C (425°F/gas mark 7).
   Place the octopus and some of the marinade into a large baking dish. Reserve the rest of the marinade. Roast the octopus for 15 minutes. While the octopus is roasting, blanch the spinach in a large saucepan and drain well.
   Divide the spinach among 6 warmed dinner plates. Place the octopus and its sauce onto the spinach. Top with the roasted red peppers. Serve immediately.

Note: If there is not enough sauce left in the baking dish when serving, place the remaining marinade into a small saucepan and boil to reduce before serving with the octopus.

ROAST BLUE-EYE COD WITH SWEET POTATO SKORDALIA AND BEETROOT

Bagaliaros Freskos me Gliki Skordalia ke Panzaria

SWEET POTATO SKORDALIA
500 g (1 lb) orange sweet potato (kumara), peeled and diced
3 cloves garlic, finely chopped
juice of 1 lemon
salt and freshly ground white pepper, to taste
225 mL (7 fl oz) virgin olive oil
100 mL (3 fl oz) milk

ROAST BLUE-EYE COD
6 blue-eye or other cod fillets, each 225 g (7 oz), boned, with the skin left intact
virgin olive oil, as needed
salt and freshly ground black pepper, to taste

BEETROOT
1 bunch of beetroot (beets), wrapped in foil and roasted in a 160°C (325°F/gas mark 3) oven for 1 hour until tender (reserve leaves if using)
¼ cup (60 mL/2 fl oz) virgin olive oil
juice of ½ lemon
salt, freshly ground black pepper and ground allspice, to taste
reserved leaves of 1 bunch of beetroot or 1 bunch of silver beet (Swiss chard), trimmed and blanched

Serves 6

THIS RECIPE REFLECTS what I think Greek cuisine is all about — clean, simple flavours and the bringing together of the produce of the earth and the sea.

Sweet Potato Skordalia: Boil the sweet potato in a large saucepan until tender. Drain. Process the sweet potato, garlic, lemon juice, salt and pepper in an electric blender or food processor until smooth. With the motor running, slowly pour in the oil, then pour in the milk. Keep the skordalia warm until needed.

Blue-Eye Cod: Preheat the oven to 200°C (425°F/gas mark 7). Heat a large frying pan or skillet until it is very hot. Brush the cod with olive oil and season with salt and pepper. Place in the pan skin side down and fry for only 1 minute. Now place in a baking dish and roast in the oven for 8 minutes.

Beetroot: Cut the beetroot into small pieces and place in a bowl with any gathered juices from the foil. Stir in the olive oil and lemon juice, and season with salt, pepper and allspice.

To Serve: Have 6 warmed serving plates ready. Reheat the greens and place some on each plate. Top with a piece of cod. Surround with the beetroot and its sauce, and place a large spoonful of skordalia on top of the cod. Serve immediately.

MEAT AND POULTRY

FOR THE AVERAGE GREEK, meat of any kind has always been expensive because of the lack of good grazing land in Greece itself. This harsh economic fact forced people to use small amounts of meat in their cooking. Instead of this being a deterrent to good cuisine, it became a challenge.

Since ancient times, Greeks have been adept at presenting meats such as pork in a variety of forms — dried, salted, smoked and so on — with almost all of the animal being eaten, including the ears, tongue and brain. Even today, little of such an animal is wasted, with most of the meat cooked or cured so that it lasts throughout winter.

In Greece, with spring comes Easter, and with Easter comes lamb and kid. Easter is the most important date in the Greek Orthodox calendar and, on the mainland, especially around central Greece, spit-roasting a tender young lamb or kid on Easter Sunday is a normal occurrence.

Spit-roasting and grilling over an open fire have been an integral part of Greek life for centuries. Equipment for ancient 'barbecues' has been found on Minoan archaeological sites. So common to Greek cuisine has this style of cooking become that souvlaki stands can be found on almost every street corner, selling souvlaki day and night.

Greeks are enormously fond of poultry, especially chicken and quail, and prepare it in many ways. Whether simply roasted with oregano and lemon, cooked in pilafs or found in stews, poultry is well loved.

As for other wild fowl and game, they, too, have been loved by Greeks since antiquity. Rabbit, the most common of game meats, is enjoyed throughout Greece and served in many different guises. One of the most unusual dishes I have come across is pickled rabbit, a speciality from the island of Crete, which unfortunately I have no recipe for.

GRILLED CHICKEN WITH ALMOND GARLIC SAUCE

Kotopoulo Stin Skara me Skordalia

GRILLED CHICKEN

3 cornfed chickens, each 1 kg (2 lb)
juice of 1 lemon
⅓ cup (90 mL/3 fl oz) extra virgin
  olive oil
1 tablespoon dried Greek
  (Mediterranean) oregano
½ cup (125 mL/4 fl oz) retsina or
  other dry white wine
2 cloves garlic, finely chopped
1 large brown (yellow) onion,
  coarsely chopped
salt and freshly ground black
  pepper, to taste

ALMOND GARLIC SAUCE

1¼ cups (125 g/4 oz) ground
  almonds
½ cup (30 g/1 oz) fresh
  breadcrumbs
6 cloves garlic, chopped
salt and freshly ground white
  pepper, to taste
juice of 1 lemon
225 mL (7 fl oz) extra virgin
  olive oil
1 tablespoon aged red wine vinegar,
  or to taste

Serves 6

THIS SAUCE WAS one of the first skordalias made by Greeks and can be traced back 2500 years. It is still made today, but more often than not just with breadcrumbs, or only a very small amount of nuts.

Grilled Chicken: Cut each chicken along the backbone and remove all of the excess bones. Flatten the chickens by pressing down on the breasts firmly with the palms of your hands.

Place the lemon juice, olive oil, oregano, wine, garlic, onion, salt and pepper in an electic blender or food processor. Process into a smooth purée. Pour this purée over the chickens, rubbing it into the chicken as you do so. Leave to marinate, preferably overnight.

Wipe any excess marinade off the chicken. Grill on a hot barbecue or grill plate for approximately 40 minutes, turning the chicken every 10 minutes. Allow to rest for 10 minutes before serving with the Almond Garlic Sauce.

Almond Garlic Sauce: Place the almonds, breadcrumbs, garlic, salt and pepper in an electric blender or food processor. Process for 10 seconds. Whisk the lemon juice and half the olive oil in a bowl and, with the motor running, slowly add to the almond mixture. When incorporated, slowly add the remaining oil, still with the motor running. If necessary, adjust the seasoning with some red wine vinegar. This sauce can be served immediately or refrigerated for up to 2 days before use.

CUMIN AND OREGANO CRUSTED VEAL FILLET WITH TOMATO SALTSA AND OLIVE ORZO

Mosharaki Filleto me Saltsa ke Manestra me Elies

6 veal tenderloin fillets, each 225 g (7 oz), trimmed
1 teaspoon cumin seeds, dry-roasted and crushed
1 teaspoon dried Greek (Mediterranean) oregano
freshly ground black pepper, to taste
olive oil, as needed
Roast Tomato Saltsa (see page 35)

OLIVE ORZO
500 g (1 lb) orzo or other rice-shaped pasta
225 g (7 oz) kalamata olives, pitted and chopped
¼ cup (60 mL/2 fl oz) extra virgin olive oil
salt and freshly ground black pepper, to taste

Serves 6

ORZO IS A TYPE OF rice-shaped pasta often sold in Greek or Middle Eastern grocery stores. The smallest orzo is no larger than short-grain rice, while the largest is the size of rockmelon (cantaloupe) seeds.

Preheat the oven to 200°C (400°F/gas mark 6).

Make sure the veal fillets are trimmed of sinew and all visible fat. Mix the cumin, oregano and pepper together well in a small bowl. Roll the veal in this seasoning, making sure to cover both sides.

Heat some olive oil in a large frying pan or skillet until quite hot. Add the seasoned veal and quickly brown on both sides to seal in the juices. Place in a baking dish and roast in the oven for 10 minutes. Remove and allow to rest, covered, for 10 minutes. Meanwhile, prepare the Olive Orzo.

Olive Orzo: Bring a large saucepan of salted water to the boil. Add the pasta and cook until tender. Drain and toss with the olives, olive oil, salt and pepper.

To Serve: Divide the Olive Orzo among 6 serving plates. Place a veal fillet on top of each serving, with the Roast Tomato Saltsa poured around the edge of each plate.

FETA-STUFFED RACK OF LAMB WITH FAVA AND ROAST GARLIC

Arni Yemisto me Feta ke Fava ke me Psito Skordo

ROAST GARLIC
*2 heads of garlic, cloves separated
    and peeled*
a little olive oil

FAVA
*250 g (8 oz) dried broad (fava)
    beans, soaked overnight in cold
    water, drained and rinsed well*
100 mL (3 fl oz) virgin olive oil
*1 brown (yellow) onion, finely
    chopped*
2 cloves garlic, finely chopped
1 small carrot, finely chopped
1 stalk celery, finely chopped
*small handful of fresh flat-leaf
    (Italian) parsley, finely chopped*
*salt and freshly ground black
    pepper, to taste*
juice of 1 lemon

FETA-STUFFED RACK OF LAMB
*6 racks of lamb (4 cutlets to each
    rack), trimmed*
*100 g (3 oz) feta cheese, cut into 6
    strips approximately 1.5 cm x
    8 cm (½ in. x 3¼ in.)*
virgin olive oil, as needed
freshly ground black pepper, to taste

Serves 6

THROUGHOUT MOST OF the Mediterranean, the word *fava* refers to the broad bean. To Greeks, *fava* is a purée, commonly made with yellow split peas, made throughout the country and usually served as a winter dish. My version is made with dried broad (fava) beans and makes a lovely accompaniment to this lamb dish.

Roast Garlic: Preheat the oven to 150°C (300°F/ gas mark 2). Coat the garlic cloves with olive oil and place in a baking dish. Bake in the oven for about 40 minutes. Set aside and keep warm.

Fava: Place the beans in a large saucepan and cover with cold water. Bring to the boil, then simmer for 30–40 minutes, until soft. Drain the beans, reserving 1 cup (250 mL/8 fl oz) of the cooking liquid. When the beans are cool to the touch, remove their skins.

Heat half of the olive oil in a large frying pan or skillet. Sauté the onion, garlic, carrot and celery over a low heat for 15 minutes, until golden in colour.

Stir in the parsley, beans, reserved cooking liquid, salt and pepper. Cook for a further 2 minutes.

Place the mixture in an electric blender or food processor with the lemon juice. Process until smooth. Slowly add the remaining olive oil and adjust the seasoning if necessary. Set aside and keep warm.

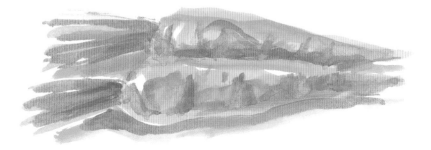

Feta-stuffed Rack of Lamb: Make a slit lengthwise through the eye or centre of each rack of lamb. Push a piece of feta into each of the openings. Coat the lamb with olive oil and pepper. Refrigerate until needed.

Preheat the oven to 200°C (400°F/gas mark 6).

Heat a large frying pan or skillet until very hot. Add a little olive oil and quickly brown the racks of lamb in the pan to seal in the juices. Place the lamb in a baking dish and bake in the oven for about 10 minutes. Set aside for 10 minutes to rest.

Have 6 warmed dinner plates ready. Divide the *fava* among the plates, placing it in the centre of each. Carve each rack into 4 slices and place on top of the *fava*. Serve with the roast garlic.

RED BRAISED DUCK WITH QUINCES

Papia Kokkinisti me Kidonia

¼ cup (60 mL/2 fl oz) olive oil
4 brown (yellow) onions, chopped
2 cloves garlic, chopped
9 duck marylands (legs with
*   thighs), trimmed of fat and*
*   separated at joint between leg*
*   and thigh*
1 tablespoon red wine vinegar
1 teaspoon cumin seeds, lightly
*   roasted and crushed*
1 stick cinnamon
1 teaspoon paprika
¼ teaspoon ground cloves
1 kg (2 lb) ripe tomatoes, peeled,
*   seeded and chopped*
1 cup (250 mL/8 fl oz) red wine
1 cup (250 mL/8 fl oz) chicken
*   stock*
2 quinces, peeled and roughly
*   chopped*
1 cup (250 mL/8 fl oz) water
1 cup (250 g/8 oz) sugar
juice of 2 lemons
1 quince (extra), peeled and
*   roughly chopped*
salt and freshly ground black
*   pepper, to taste*

Serves 6

BRAISING QUICNES WITH meat or poultry, as in this recipe, typifies the rich cuisine of northern Greece. Quinces were once used in very much the same way as potatoes are used today. Even the term *kidonáto* (another name for this braise) refers to cutting potatoes up 'quince style'.

Heat the olive oil in a large, heavy saucepan. Add the onion and garlic, and cook until golden in colour. Add the duck pieces to the pan and brown well. Remove the duck pieces and deglaze the saucepan with the red wine vinegar.

Return the duck to the pan and add the cumin seeds, cinnamon, paprika, cloves, tomato, wine, stock and quince. Bring to the boil, then simmer slowly for 2–3 hours.

While the duck is cooking, place the water, sugar and lemon juice in a small pan. Bring to the boil. Add the extra quince pieces and simmer gently for about 1–2 hours, until the quince is very tender and a brilliant red colour. Add to the braised duck just before serving, stir well and season with salt and pepper. Serve immediately.

KEFALONIAN RABBIT AND BLACK OLIVE PIE
Kounelopitta Apo Tin Kefalonia

a little virgin olive oil
1 medium-sized white rabbit,
    cleaned and cut into 6 portions
2 medium brown (yellow) onions,
    finely chopped
6 cloves garlic, finely chopped
1 cup (250 mL/8 fl oz) red wine
1 kg (2 lb) ripe tomatoes, peeled,
    seeded and chopped
1 teaspoon dried Greek
    (Mediterranean) oregano
½ stick cinnamon
sugar, salt and freshly ground
    black pepper, to taste
150 g (5 oz) kalamata olives, pitted
    and halved
handful of fresh flat-leaf (Italian)
    parsley, chopped
6 fresh mint leaves, chopped
8 thick sheets filo pastry
¼ cup (60 g/2 oz) butter, melted

Serves 6

THIS IS A KEFALONIAN-INSPIRED dish that is traditionally made with hare. Kefalonia is one of the Ionian Islands and is known throughout Greece for its highly original cuisine.

Heat a little olive oil in a large frying pan or skillet. Add the rabbit portions and brown quickly on all sides. Transfer the rabbit to a large saucepan, leaving the oil in the pan. Now add the onion to the oil and sauté until golden in colour. Add the onion to the rabbit along with the garlic, wine, tomatoes, oregano, cinnamon, sugar, salt and pepper. Bring to the boil and simmer for 1 hour.

Allow the rabbit to cool. Take the meat off the bones and shred it. Discard the bones and remove the cinnamon stick from the sauce. Stir the rabbit meat back into the sauce and add the olives, parsley and mint. Allow the rabbit filling to cool completely.

Preheat the oven to 180°C (350°F/gas mark 4). Grease a 20 cm (8 in.) pie pan and set aside.

Brush the sheets of filo with the melted butter and place into 2 stacks of 4 sheets. Cut each stack to fit the pie pan, with the base sheets cut larger than the top ones. Place the base sheets of filo into the pan and pour in the rabbit filling. Cover with the top sheets of filo and gather the edges of the pastry together firmly. Brush the top of the pie with melted butter and bake in the oven for about 40 minutes. Serve.

ROAST BABY CHICKENS WITH PINE NUT, FETA AND RICE STUFFING

Kotopoulakia Yemista me Koukounaria, Feta ke Risi

ROAST BABY CHICKENS
¼ cup (60 mL/2 fl oz) virgin
   olive oil
juice of 1 lemon
1 tablespoon brandy
1 tablespoon chopped fresh thyme
   leaves
salt and freshly ground black
   pepper, to taste
6 baby chickens or spatchcocks
   (Cornish game hens), each
   500 g (1 lb), tunnel boned (ask
   your butcher or poultry supplier
   to do this)
butcher's string, to tie the birds

PINE NUT, FETA AND RICE
   STUFFING
¼ cup (60 mL/2 fl oz) olive oil
1 brown (yellow) onion, finely
   chopped
2 cloves garlic, finely chopped
1½ cups (250 g/8 oz) long-grain
   rice
2 cups (500 mL/16 fl oz) chicken
   stock
1 teaspoon dried oregano
100 g (3 oz) pine nuts, lightly
   toasted
225 g (7 oz) mild feta cheese
handful of fresh flat-leaf (Italian)
   parsley, finely chopped
salt and freshly ground black
   pepper, to taste
1 egg, lightly beaten

THIS DISH IS ADAPTED from a recipe from the northern state of Thrace, near the Albanian border with Greece. It is best to use a mild young feta for the filling so as not to overpower the subtle flavours of the dish.

Whisk the olive oil, lemon juice, brandy, thyme, salt and pepper together in a bowl. Place the chickens or spatchcocks in a glass or ceramic bowl. Pour the marinade over the top. Cover and refrigerate for at least 2 hours.

Pine Nut, Feta and Rice Stuffing: Heat the olive oil in a large saucepan over a moderate heat. Add the onion and garlic, and sauté until they are translucent. Add the rice and cook for another minute, stirring continuously. Now add the stock and oregano. Reduce the heat and simmer until the liquid has been absorbed into the mixture. Remove from the heat, cover with a clean cloth and a lid, and allow to rest for 10 minutes.

Put the rice mixture into a large bowl. Stir in the pine nuts, feta, parsley, salt and pepper. Allow to cool. Stir in the egg to bind the stuffing together well.

TO SERVE
*4 red capsicum (bell peppers),
    roasted, peeled, seeded and cut
    into thick strips, tossed in some
    olive oil (see page 38)*

Serves 6

To Assemble the Dish: Preheat the oven to 200°C (400°F/gas mark 6).

Remove the chickens or spatchcocks from the marinade, draining well. Reserve the marinade. Wipe the chickens or spatchcocks with paper towels or absorbent kitchen paper. Fill the cavity of each chicken or spatchcock with some stuffing. Use the butcher's string to close the cavity and hold the stuffing in place. Place the chickens or spatchcocks in a large baking dish. Pour the marinade over the top. Bake in the oven for 40 minutes.

To Serve: Divide the roasted capsicum among 6 serving plates. Place a chicken or spatchcock on each bed of capsicum. Serve immediately.

BRAISED PIGEON WITH ARTICHOKES

Pistounia me Anginares

virgin olive oil, as needed

*6 squab (pigeons), cleaned and
    halved*

*1 large brown (yellow) onion, finely
    chopped*

*3 large ripe tomatoes, peeled,
    seeded and finely chopped*

*1 cup (250 mL/8 fl oz) rich
    chicken stock*

*12 young globe artichokes,
    trimmed of tough outer leaves,
    halved and soaked in acidulated
    water* (reserve the stalks for the
    skordalia)*

*½ small bunch of fresh dill, stalks
    removed and leaves finely
    chopped*

*½ small bunch of fresh flat-leaf
    (Italian) parsley, stalks removed
    and leaves finely chopped*

*salt and freshly ground black
    pepper, to taste*

ARTICHOKE SKORDALIA

*reserved artichoke stalks, trimmed,
    peeled and chopped*

*250 g (8 oz) Jerusalem artichokes,
    peeled and chopped*

*1 head of garlic, cloves peeled and
    blanched*

juice of 1 lemon

*100 mL (3 fl oz) extra virgin
    olive oil*

¼ cup (60 mL/2 fl oz) milk

*salt and freshly ground white
    pepper, to taste*

Serves 6

THIS RECIPE MAKES the perfect winter dish — rich and full of flavour. Squabs are young and tender domesticated pigeons, and are available either fresh or frozen depending upon the time of year. Both the squab and the artichoke are braised slowly in this recipe to develop flavour and tenderness.

Heat some olive oil in a large saucepan and brown the squab in batches. Remove to a covered plate and keep warm.

Now sauté the onion in the same pan until golden in colour. Return the squab and its juices to the pan with the onion. Add the tomatoes and stock, bring to the boil and simmer for 45 minutes. Add the artichoke halves and simmer for 15 minutes. Stir in the dill, parsley, salt and pepper. Simmer for another 15 minutes.

Serve in large soup plates on top of a large dollop of the Artichoke Skordalia, which will absorb some of the sauce.

Artichoke Skordalia: Bring a large saucepan of salted water to the boil. Add the artichoke stalks, Jerusalem artichokes and garlic. Cook until tender, about 20 minutes.

Drain off the water and place the vegetables in an electric blender or food processor with the lemon juice and half the olive oil. Purée until smooth, slowly adding the rest of the olive oil with the motor still running. Slowly add the milk and adjust the seasoning with salt and pepper. Keep warm until ready to serve.

*Acidulated water is made by adding a small amount of vinegar, lemon juice or lime juice to water. It helps to prevent discoloration.

POT-ROASTED SQUAB WITH OREGANO AND TOMATOES

Pistounia Stin Katsarola me Rigani ke Tomates

*150 mL (5 fl oz) extra virgin
  olive oil*
*6 squab (pigeons), cleaned, with
  the wing tips trimmed*
*1 tablespoon dried Greek
  (Mediterranean) oregano*
*400 mL (13 fl oz) dry white wine
  (such as retsina)*
*1 kg (2 lb) egg (plum) tomatoes,
  peeled and left whole*
*salt and freshly ground black
  pepper, to taste*
*6 thick slices chewy, country-style
  bread*
a little olive oil

Serves 6

METEORA IS A VERY BEAUTIFUL part of central Greece, famous for its monasteries, which almost seem to be carved into the tops of the mountains they perch upon. I would have to say that this area should also be famous for this dish, which I enjoyed with a couple of bottles of Metsovon Cabernet the evening I spent there.

Heat the olive oil in a large saucepan. Brown the squab on all sides, then add the oregano and half of the wine. Reduce the heat to very low, cover the pan and cook the squab until the wine has been absorbed.

Turn the squab over and add the remaining wine. Keep the pan covered and cook until all the wine has evaporated. Add the tomatoes to the pan and season with salt and pepper. Cook until the tomatoes have softened, but not broken up, about 20–25 minutes.

Meanwhile, brush the bread slices with olive oil and grill or broil on both sides until lightly browned.

Place a slice of grilled bread on each plate and top with some tomatoes. Halve each squab and place on top of the tomatoes. Pour over the pan juices and serve immediately.

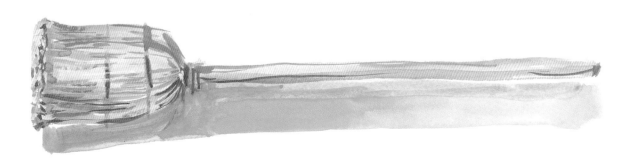

HERBED CHICKEN BREASTS WITH POTATO AND CAPER PURÉE

Kotopoulo Stithos me Patata Poure ke Kapares

HERBED CHICKEN BREASTS
3 tablespoons plain yoghurt
1 clove garlic, finely chopped
2 tablespoons finely chopped fresh
   flat-leaf (Italian) parsley
1 tablespoon finely chopped fresh
   thyme
salt and freshly ground black
   pepper, to taste
6 chicken breast fillets, boned (with
   skin left on) and cleaned
extra virgin olive oil, as needed

POTATO AND CAPER PURÉE
1 kg (2 lb) waxy (boiling) potatoes
   (such as desirée or pontiac),
   peeled and diced
100 g (3 oz) capers, soaked in cold
   water (salt-preserved capers are
   best)
juice of 2 lemons
225 mL (7 fl oz) extra virgin
   olive oil
salt and freshly ground black
   pepper, to taste
100 mL (3 fl oz) milk, warmed

TO FINISH THE DISH
1 bunch of chicory, trimmed of
   tough stalks, washed and dried
a little olive oil
150 mL (5 fl oz) dry white wine

Serves 6

POTATOES FIRST ARRIVED in Greece just after the revolution of the nineteenth century, and have remained a popular and versatile vegetable in Greek cooking ever since. The purée in this dish is also delicious partnered with pan-fried slices of calf's or lamb's liver and a squeeze of lemon juice.

Herbed Chicken Breasts: Mix the yoghurt, garlic, parsley, thyme, salt and pepper together well in a small bowl.

Gently separate the skin from the chicken breasts, leaving it attached on one side. Spread a spoonful of herb paste over each breast fillet then cover with the skin.

Brush each fillet with a little olive oil and season with pepper. Set aside in the refrigerator for 30 minutes.

Potato and Caper Purée: Bring a large saucepan of salted water to the boil. Add the potatoes and cook until they are tender.

Meanwhile, purée the capers, lemon juice, olive oil, salt and pepper in an electric blender or food processor.

Drain the potatoes and pass them through a food mill into a bowl. Pour in the caper mixture and beat in well. Now pour in the milk and beat until the potatoes are light and fluffy. Set aside and keep warm.

To Finish the Dish: Preheat the oven to 200°C (400°F/gas mark 6).

Heat a large frying pan or skillet until very hot. Place the chicken fillets, skin side down, in the pan. Cook for 1 minute. Remove the fillets from the pan and place in a baking dish skin side up. Bake in the oven for 10–12 minutes.

Meanwhile, bring a large saucepan of water to the boil. Add the chicory and cook for 2–3 minutes. Drain well and toss with a little olive oil.

To Serve: Divide the Potato and Caper Purée among 6 warmed dinner plates. Place some chicory on top of each serving of purée and then top each serving with a chicken breast.

Use the white wine to deglaze the dish the chicken was baked in. Pour some of this sauce over each chicken breast. Serve immediately.

QUAIL-STUFFED EGGPLANT, 'KLEPHTIC' STYLE

Ortikia Klephtika se Melitzanes

6 firm medium eggplant
   (aubergines)
150 mL (5 fl oz) extra virgin
   olive oil
2 medium brown (yellow) onions,
   finely chopped
4 cloves garlic, finely chopped
500 g (1 lb) ripe tomatoes, peeled,
   seeded and chopped
225 mL (7 fl oz) white wine
1 teaspoon dried oregano
¼ teaspoon ground cinnamon
salt, freshly ground black pepper
   and sugar, to taste
9 quails, quartered and trimmed
   of back bones
1 large red capsicum (bell pepper),
   roasted, peeled and cut into thin
   strips (see page 38)
300 g (10 oz) golden shallots,
   peeled and deep-fried whole
   until golden
extra virgin olive oil
Roast Tomato Saltsa (see page 35)

Serves 6

THIS DISH IS ADAPTED from one popular on the eastern Aegean islands of Greece and throughout Cyprus. The term *khlephtic* refers to the bandits who, during the War of Independence, would turn up in villages at meal times, after searching out the aromas of food cooking. This style of cooking was created almost as a means of protection against these bandits, with the meat being sealed in a casing before being baked so that very little of the aroma escaped.

Preheat the oven to 180°C (350°F/gas mark 4). Place the eggplants on a baking sheet and rub with a little olive oil. Bake for 6–8 minutes, until they soften a little. Remove from the oven and allow to cool.

   Carefully cut off the top third of each eggplant lengthwise and set aside. Hollow out the eggplants, reserving the pulp for another use. Brush the inside of each hollowed eggplant with some olive oil. Set aside.

   Heat 100 mL (3 fl oz) of the olive oil in a large, heavy saucepan over a low heat. Add the onion and garlic, and cook for about 10 minutes, until golden in colour. Add the tomato, white wine, oregano, cinnamon, salt, pepper and sugar. Simmer for 10 minutes.

   Heat the remaining olive oil in a large frying pan. Add the quail pieces and brown on all sides. Now add the quail to the tomato mixture, along with the capsicum and shallots.

   Place the eggplant shells in a greased baking dish. Divide the quail mixture among the eggplants, reserving some liquid. Top each eggplant with its matching 'lid'. Pour the reserved liquid around the eggplant in the baking dish and bake in the oven for 30 minutes. Serve immediately, accompanied by the Roast Tomato Saltsa and the baking juices.

SLOW-BRAISED BEEF CHUCK WITH ARTICHOKES AND PINE NUTS

Kreas me Anginares ke Koukounaria

2 tablespoons virgin olive oil

1.5 kg (3 lb) beef chuck

6 cloves garlic, peeled and cut into
    thin slices

½ teaspoon cumin seeds, dry-
    roasted and finely ground

2½ cups (625 mL/1 imp. pint)
    rich beef stock

salt and freshly ground black
    pepper, to taste

12 globe artichokes, topped,
    trimmed of tough outer leaves,
    stalks peeled and quartered

150 g (5 oz) pine nuts

juice of 1 lemon

Serves 6

ACCORDING TO GREEK LEGEND, the artichoke came from an island in the Aegean known as Zinari. On this island there lived a beautiful girl named Kinara who was admired by all the men who lived there. Unfortunately, this so enraged a jealous goddess that she turned Kinara into an artichoke.

I love artichokes and this is one of my favourite ways to serve them. It is also quite an economical meal to prepare when artichokes are in season, as the meat used is an inexpensive but flavourful cut.

Heat the olive oil in a large casserole dish and brown the beef on all sides. Add the garlic and sauté until golden. Add the cumin, stock, salt and pepper. Cover and simmer over a low heat for 2 hours. Add the artichokes, pine nuts and lemon juice. Simmer for 30–40 minutes. Remove the beef and slice. Serve with the some of the artichokes on each plate, and the sauce poured over the top.

LAMB'S LIVER WITH OREGANO AND LEMON
Sikotakia Tiganita me Limoni

*1 kg (2 lb) lamb's or calf's liver,
    trimmed of any membrane and
    cut into 6 mm (¼ in.) slices*
*plain (all-purpose) flour, seasoned
    with salt and freshly ground
    black pepper, to coat the liver*
*150 mL (5 fl oz) extra virgin
    olive oil*
*2 tablespoon dried Greek
    (Mediterranean) oregano*
juice of 2 lemons
*1 tablespoon preserved lemon,
    finely chopped (see page 111)*
½ teaspoon ground cumin
*salt and freshly ground black
    pepper, to taste*
*handful of roughly chopped fresh
    flat-leaf (Italian) parsley*
*Potato and Caper Purée (see
    page 82)*

Serves 6

THIN SLICES OF LAMB'S LIVER lightly sautéed and dressed with lemon juice is a classic of Greek cuisine. Most tavernas throughout Greece serve small portions of this dish as part of a *mezethes*. At Cosmos, I like to serve thicker slices of liver, cooked until pink inside, as a main course, usually on a bed of Potato and Caper Purée and sprinkled with deep-fried capers.

Lightly dust the liver pieces with the seasoned flour. Heat 100 mL (3 fl oz) of the olive oil in a large frying pan or skillet. Add the liver and sauté for 1–2 minutes on each side. Set aside and keep warm.

Add the remaining olive oil, oregano, lemon juice, preserved lemon, cumin, salt, pepper and parsley to the pan. Cook for a few seconds.

Divide the Potato and Caper Purée among 6 warmed dinner plates. Top with the liver pieces and pour some of the sauce over each serving. Serve immediately.

SPIT-ROASTED BABY LAMB OR KID

Arnaki i Katsikaki Sti Souvla

1 whole baby lamb or kid, about
   5-6 kg (10-12 lb), with the
   innards removed and the
   carcass cleaned

MARINADE
juice of 2 lemons
2 cups (500 mL/16 fl oz) extra
   virgin olive oil
1 tablespoon dried Greek
   (Mediterranean) oregano
2 onions, sliced
4 cloves garlic, lightly crushed with
   the blade of a knife
4 bay leaves, crumbled
salt and freshly ground black
   pepper, to taste
white wine, to cover the lamb
   or kid

Serves 10-16

SPIT-ROASTED BABY LAMB or goat has come to be known as the classic Easter meal throughout the mainland of Greece, especially around Koumeli, in central Greece. If the carcass is left to marinate for at least 24 hours, the flavour is sublime.

Place the carcass in a vessel large enough to contain it. Mix all the marinade ingredients together and pour over the lamb or kid. Refrigerate and leave to marinate for at least 24 hours. Drain off the marinade and reserve.

Pat the lamb or kid dry with paper towels or absorbent kitchen paper. Pass the spit skewer through the carcass and tie the legs together securely with string. Follow the manufacturer's instructions for securing and roasting with a spit-roaster.

Roast the lamb or kid over slow-burning coals. The fire should be started 2–3 hours before cooking. Roast for at least 4 hours, basting every 30 minutes with the reserved marinade, until the skin becomes a rich, dark brown colour and the meat can be pulled away from the bones easily.

Carefully remove the lamb or kid from the skewer and carve into slices to serve.

LAMB SHANK PIE

Arnisia Kotsia Pitta

100 mL (3 fl oz) virgin olive oil
8 lamb shanks, trimmed of sinew
    and excess fat
2 large brown (yellow) onions,
    finely chopped
2 stalks celery, finely chopped
2 cloves garlic, finely chopped
1 kg (2 lb) ripe tomatoes, peeled,
    seeded and chopped
1¼ cups (300 mL/10 fl oz) lamb
    or chicken stock
salt, freshly ground black pepper
    and sugar, to taste
½ teaspoon ground cinnamon
1 bunch of fresh flat-leaf (Italian)
    parsley, stalks discarded and
    leaves finely chopped

PASTRY
6 cups (750 g/1½ lb) plain (all-
    purpose) flour
1 teaspoon salt
¼ cup (60 mL (2 fl oz) virgin
    olive oil
1 egg, lightly beaten
¼ cup (60 mL/2 fl oz) iced water

TO ASSEMBLE THE PIE
4 eggs
150 g (5 oz) kefalotyri or mild
    Parmesan cheese, grated
1 cup cooked rice
1 egg yolk, beaten with
    1 tablespoon water, to glaze pie

Serves 6–8

THIS PIE ORIGINATES FROM northern Greece, where it is traditionally made during Carnivale and on Ascension Day, which is the fortieth day after Easter Sunday. On Ascension Day in Greece, a special Divine Liturgy is held to commemorate Christ's last appearance on Earth.

Heat the olive oil in a large, heavy saucepan over a moderate heat. Add the lamb shanks and brown on all sides. Remove the shanks from the saucepan and set aside. Reduce the heat to low and add the onion, celery and garlic. Sauté for 10 minutes, until golden in colour. Return the shanks to the saucepan.

Add the tomatoes, stock, salt, pepper, sugar and cinnamon. Simmer gently for 1½ hours, until the meat comes off the bone easily and the sauce has thickened. Allow to cool slightly, then take the meat off the bones and return it to the saucepan. Discard the bones. Stir the parsley into the meat mixture. Set aside and cool.

Pastry: Place all the ingredients for the pastry in an electric blender or food processor. Process until the mixture forms into a ball. Wrap the pastry in plastic wrap (cling film) and chill for at least 1 hour.

To Assemble the Pie: Preheat the oven to 190°C (375°F/gas mark 5).

Beat the eggs lightly in a small bowl and add the *kefalotyri* or Parmesan. Stir into the meat mixture along with the rice.

Divide the pastry into 2 balls, one slightly larger than the other. Grease a large baking sheet. On a lightly floured surface, roll each piece of pastry into a circle, about 5 mm (¼ in.) thick, one 30 cm (12 in.) in diameter, the other 25 cm (10 in.). Place the larger circle on the baking sheet. Spread the meat filling onto the pastry base, leaving a 2.5 cm (1 in.) rim around the outside to seal the pastry edges. Cover with the other sheet of pastry. Gather and pinch the edges of the pastry together to form a fluted rim. Brush the top of the pie with the egg glaze.

Bake in the oven for about 40 minutes, until the crust is crisp and golden. Serve cut into wedges.

KID BACKSTRAP FILLET WITH SMOKED EGGPLANT SALATA AND ZUCCHINI

Katsikaki Filleto me Melitzanosalata ke Kolokithakia

6 kid backstrap fillets or lamb loin
    fillets, each 185 g (6 oz),
    trimmed
virgin olive oil, as needed
1 teaspoon dried Greek
    (Mediterranean) oregano
1 teaspoon freshly cracked black
    pepper

SMOKED EGGPLANT SALATA
3 medium eggplant (aubergines)
1 small sweet white onion, finely
    chopped
2 cloves garlic, finely chopped
1 large, ripe tomato, peeled, seeded
    and chopped
1 teaspoon dried Greek
    (Mediterranean) oregano
small handful of fresh flat-leaf
    (Italian) parsley, leaves chopped
juice of 1 lemon
salt and freshly ground black
    pepper, to taste
¼ cup (60 mL/2 fl oz) extra virgin
    olive oil

9 small zucchini (courgettes),
    preferably with blossom
    attached
virgin olive oil, as needed

Serves 6

THE SMOKY FLAVOUR OF the eggplant purée in this recipe works well with the richness of the kid or lamb. If you prefer a more subtle flavour, simply bake the eggplant for about 30 minutes instead of roasting or grilling it, then make the salata as given.

Preheat the oven to 190°C (375°F/gas mark 5).

Place the kid or lamb fillets in a shallow bowl and marinate with some olive oil, the oregano and pepper. Cover and refrigerate for at least 1 hour.

Hold the eggplant over a direct flame on a gas stove or grill on a preheated grill plate. Cook until the skin blackens and blisters, turning the eggplant around every 2 minutes. Place in the oven for 5 minutes, until they are very soft. Allow to cool.

Peel the skin off the eggplant (you can do this under cold running water) and remove the seeds. Squeeze the pulp to extract the bitter juices. Place the eggplant pulp in a blender or food processor. Add the onion, garlic, tomato, oregano, parsley, lemon juice, salt and pepper. Process into a smooth purée. With the motor still running, slowly add the olive oil. Set aside and keep warm.

Heat a frying pan or skillet over a moderate heat. Brown the kid or lamb fillets on all sides to seal in the juices. Place the fillets in a baking dish and roast in the oven for 6 minutes. They should be quite pink.

While the fillets are roasting, slice the zucchini in half lengthwise and brush with olive oil. Grill or broil on both sides until browned.

Carve the kid or lamb fillets into several slices. Divide the Smoked Eggplant Salata among 6 preheated dinner plates. Top each serving with the sliced kid or lamb fillets and 3 zucchini halves. Serve immediately.

LAMB LOIN WITH ROAST BEETROOT AND RADISH TZATZIKI

Arni me Panzaria ke Tzatziki Rapanakia

LAMB LOIN

6 trimmed lamb loins or thick
lamb fillets, each 225 g (7 oz)
2 tablespoons virgin olive oil
freshly ground black pepper, to taste

RADISH TZATZIKI

1 bunch red radishes, washed,
roots trimmed and grated
1 small red onion, grated
3 cloves garlic, finely chopped
1 tablespoon red wine vinegar
½ teaspoon sugar
½ teaspoon salt
freshly ground white pepper, to
taste
1 cup (250 mL/8 fl oz) plain
yoghurt

ROAST BEETROOT

12 small beetroot (beets), with
leaves
1 small red onion, finely chopped
juice of 1 lemon
⅓ cup (90 mL/3 fl oz) extra virgin
olive oil
salt and freshly ground black
pepper, to taste

Serves 6

TRY TO BUY BEETROOT (beets) with their crisp, green and burgundy-veined leaves still attached. These leaves are packed with lots of essential vitamins and minerals.

Lamb Loin: Roll the lamb in the olive oil and pepper. Cover with plastic wrap (cling film) and refrigerate for 2 hours.

Radish Tzatziki: Mix the ingredients for the tzatziki together. Cover and refrigerate for 1 hour.

Roast Beetroot: Preheat the oven to 160°C (325°F/gas mark 3). Trim the beetroot leaves from the beetroot. Wash and drain the leaves. Set aside.

Peel the beetroot and wrap in aluminium foil. Roast in the oven until tender, about 30–40 minutes. Remove from the foil and cut into quarters, taking care to keep any juices that have accumulated in the foil. Increase the oven temperature to 220°C (425°F/gas mark 7). Pour the beetroot into a bowl with the accumulated juices. Add the onion, half the lemon juice, half the olive oil, salt and pepper.

To Finish the Dish: Heat a frying pan or skillet until quite hot. Add the lamb and quickly brown on all sides. Place in a baking dish and roast in the oven for 8-10 minutes. Allow to rest for 10 minutes.

Bring a saucepan of salted water to the boil. Add the beetroot leaves and blanch for 1 minute. Drain well and toss with the remaining lemon juice and olive oil.

To Serve: Place some beetroot greens in the centre of 6 serving plates. Slice each lamb loin into 3 pieces and stand on top of the greens. Surround with the beetroot and top with a large spoonful of tzatziki.

BEEF 'SOFRITO' WITH ROAST GARLIC AND BITTER GREENS

Sofrito me Pisto Skordo ke Horta

1 kg (2 lb) beef rump or topside, trimmed
100 mL (3 fl oz) extra virgin olive oil
2 cups (500 mL/16 fl oz) red wine
100 mL (3 fl oz) red wine vinegar
6 cloves garlic, roughly chopped
1 tablespoon chopped fresh thyme
1 teaspoon chopped fresh rosemary
freshly ground black pepper, to taste
2 bay leaves, crumbled
virgin olive oil (extra), as needed
100 mL (3 fl oz) reduced rich veal or beef stock
salt, to taste

ROAST GARLIC
3 heads of garlic, cloves separated and peeled
¼ cup (60 mL/2 fl oz) olive oil
1 tablespoon water
salt and freshly ground black pepper, to taste

*1 bunch of chicory or curly endive (*frisée*) or thistle, trimmed, washed and drained*
extra virgin olive oil, to dress the greens

Serves 6

SOFRITO IS A SPECIALITY of Corfu. There it is made into a rich stew by slowly cooking it in clay pots, until meltingly tender.

Slice the beef lengthwise into 12 pieces. Beat out slightly with a meat mallet. Cover and refrigerate.

Add the extra virgin olive oil, red wine, red wine vinegar, garlic, thyme, rosemary, pepper and bay leaves to a saucepan. Bring to the boil and simmer for 2 minutes. Remove from the heat and allow to cool completely. Place the beef slices in this marinade and set aside for 2 hours at room temperature.

Preheat the oven to 120°C (250°F/gas mark 1/2). Place the garlic, olive oil and water in a baking dish and roast in the oven for 1 hour, until the cloves have softened and are golden in colour. Mash the garlic with a fork until smooth. Season with salt and pepper.

Bring a saucepan of salted water to the boil. Add the greens and cook for 2 minutes. Remove from the saucepan and drain well. Toss the greens with a little olive oil. Set aside and keep warm.

Remove the beef slices from the refrigerator and drain, reserving the marinade. Dry the beef well with paper towels or absorbent kitchen paper. Heat the extra olive oil in a large frying pan or skillet, and brown the beef slices for about 2 minutes on both sides. Do this in several batches, keeping the meat warm in the oven until all the slices are done.

Strain the marinade into the frying pan and add the stock. Increase the heat and boil until reduced to a syrup.

Place a slice of beef on each of 6 warmed dinner plates. Spread some roast garlic purée on top of the meat and then top with some greens. Cover with another slice of beef and pour the reduced sauce over and around the meat. Serve immediately.

BARBECUED KANGAROO SOUVLAKI WITH LEMON AND OLIVE PILAF

Souvlakia me Pilafi ke Mantanosalata

BARBECUED SOUVLAKI

2 kg (4 lb) kangaroo or venison or lamb backstrap, trimmed of sinew and cut into 2.5 cm (1 in.) cubes

12 bamboo skewers, soaked in cold water for several hours

freshly cracked black pepper, to taste

1 small bunch of fresh oregano, stems removed and leaves chopped

⅓ cup (90 mL/3 fl oz) extra virgin olive oil

LEMON AND OLIVE PILAF

¼ cup (60 mL/2 fl oz) virgin olive oil

2 cups (375 g (12 oz) arborio rice

3½ cups (875 mL/28 fl oz) chicken stock

1 bay leaf

1 teaspoon salt

grated rind of 2 lemons

juice of 1 lemon

125 g (4 oz) kalamata olives, pitted and chopped

handful of fresh flat-leaf (Italian) parsley, stems removed and leaves finely chopped

TO SERVE
Parsley Salata (see page 65)

Serves 6

KANGAROO IS A LOVELY meat with quite a delicate, sweet flavour that works perfectly in this recipe. If you cannot obtain this meat, young venison or lamb may be used instead.

Thread the cubes of meat onto the skewers, place in a flat, non-corrosive dish and marinate with the pepper, oregano and oil for 2 hours.

Heat the olive oil in a heavy saucepan over a low heat. Add the rice and cook until the rice grains whiten, about 2 minutes. Add the stock, bay leaf and salt. Increase the heat and boil, uncovered and without stirring, until the liquid has been absorbed, about 12 minutes. Remove the saucepan from the heat, cover with a clean cloth and set aside for 20 minutes. Meanwhile, barbecue the souvlaki.

Take the meat from the dish and wipe off any excess moisture. Grill on a very hot barbecue or grill plate for about 3 minutes on each side. Allow the souvlaki to rest, covered, for 10 minutes.

Stir the lemon rind, juice, olives and parsley into the pilaf. Divide the pilaf among 6 serving plates. Top each serving with 2 souvlaki, removed from the skewers, and serve with the Parsley Salata.

LAMB SHANKS WITH BROAD BEANS

Arnisia Kotsia me Koukia

⅓ cup (90 mL/3 fl oz) virgin
   olive oil
12 lamb shanks (ask your butcher
   to cut the base off each shank)
3 brown (yellow) onions, finely
   chopped
2 cloves garlic, finely chopped
1 kg (2 lb) ripe tomatoes, peeled,
   seeded and finely chopped
1 tablespoon honey
¼ cup (60 mL/2 fl oz) verjuice or
   juice of 1 lemon
½ cup (125 mL/4 fl oz) rich lamb
   or chicken stock
1 tablespoon cumin seeds, dry-
   roasted and finely ground in a
   spice mill
1 teaspoon dried Greek
   (Mediterranean) oregano
salt and freshly ground black
   pepper, to taste
1 kg (2 lb) fresh broad (fava)
   beans, shelled and skinned
1 bunch of fresh flat-leaf (Italian)
   parsley, stems removed and
   leaves coarsely chopped

Serves 6

THIS IS A POPULAR spring dish made throughout many villages in Greece, each with its own variation. Such a dish would usually be taken to the local bakery and cooked in the *fournos*, as is done with many of the villager's roast meals.

Preheat the oven to 160°C (325°F/gas mark 3).

Heat the olive oil in a large, heavy saucepan. Add the lamb shanks and brown quickly on all sides. Remove the shanks from the saucepan and place in a large casserole dish. Keep the oil in the saucepan.

Now add the onions and garlic to the oil, and sauté over a low heat until they are golden in colour. Add the tomatoes, honey, verjuice or lemon juice, stock, cumin, oregano, salt and pepper. Bring to the boil and simmer for 5 minutes, then pour over the lamb shanks.

Cover the casserole dish and bake the lamb in the oven for 1½ hours. Add the broad beans and parsley, return to the oven and bake for another 30 minutes, until very tender. Serve immediately.

PORK FILLET WITH BULGHUR AND CHICKPEAS

Hirino Filleto me Pligouri ke Revithia

6 pork fillets (tenderloin)
1 tablespoon finely chopped fresh
*   flat-leaf (Italian) parsley*
1 tablespoon finely chopped fresh
*   coriander (cilantro)*
2 tablespoons virgin olive oil
salt and freshly ground black
*   pepper, to taste*
250 g (8 oz) dried chickpeas,
*   soaked in cold water overnight,*
*   drained and rinsed well*
½ cup (125 mL/4 fl oz) virgin
*   olive oil (extra)*
2 medium brown (yellow) onions,
*   finely chopped*
500 g (1 lb) bulghur wheat
*   (burghul), rinsed and drained*
3½ cups (875 mL/28 fl oz)
*   chicken stock*
fresh coriander (cilantro) leaves, to
*   garnish*

Serves 6

GREEKS, ESPECIALLY CYPRIOTS, love bulghur wheat (burghul). It is eaten in soups and stews, and in many pilafs. The combination of pork and bulghur is quite popular among Cypriot Greeks and comes in many guises.

Place the pork fillets in a large, shallow glass or ceramic dish. Add the parsley, coriander, olive oil, salt and pepper. Combine the ingredients well. Cover and refrigerate for 2 hours.

Bring a saucepan of salted water to the boil. Add the chickpeas and cook until tender, about 1 hour. Leave to rest in the cooking liquid until needed.

Heat the extra olive oil in a large, heavy saucepan over a moderate heat. Add the onion and sauté until it is golden in colour. Add the bulghur and stir over the heat for 2–3 minutes. Reduce the heat to low. Add the stock and drained chickpeas, and season with salt and pepper. Cover and simmer for 15–20 minutes. Remove from the heat and allow to rest, covered, for another 15 minutes.

Preheat the oven to 200°C (400°F/gas mark 6).

Heat a large frying pan or skillet until quite hot. Add the pork fillets and quickly sear the meat on all sides until golden. Roast in the oven for 6–7 minutes. Remove the meat from the oven and allow to rest for 5 minutes.

Divide the bulghur mixture among 6 dinner plates. Slice each fillet into several pieces and place on top of the bulghur. Garnish with the coriander leaves and serve immediately.

ROAST BEEF RUMP WITH AUTUMN VEGETABLES AND KALAMATA OLIVES

Moschari Psito me Tourlou ke Elies

AUTUMN VEGETABLES
500 g (1 lb) okra
225 mL (7 fl oz) vinegar
1 tablespoon salt
1 kg (2 lb) roma tomatoes, peeled,
    seeded and coarsely chopped
2 onions, finely chopped
2 zucchini (courgettes), cut into
    1 cm (½ in.) cubes
2 large waxy (boiling) potatoes, cut
    into 1 cm (½ in.) cubes
6 cloves garlic, finely chopped
1 red capsicum (bell pepper),
    peeled, seeded and cut into 1 cm
    (½ in.) cubes
1 yellow capsicum (bell pepper),
    peeled, seeded and cut into 1 cm
    (½ in.) cubes
1 small bunch of fresh flat-leaf
    (Italian) parsley, stalks removed
    and leaves chopped
⅓ cup (90 mL/3 fl oz) extra virgin
    olive oil
1 cup (250 mL/8 fl oz) light beef
    stock or water, boiling
salt and freshly ground black
    pepper, to taste

AS WITH MANY GREEK vegetables dishes, this one is generally served at room temperature to bring out the flavour of the vegetables. I love to serve this dish hot with slices of rare roasted beef and shavings of *kefalotyri* cheese on top, but the baked vegetables also make a substantial vegetarian dish when served on their own.

Autumn Vegetables: Preheat the oven to 160°C (325°F/gas mark 3). Trim the top of each okra and discard. Lay the okra in a single layer in a flat dish and sprinkle with the vinegar and salt. Set aside for at least 1 hour and allow the juices to disgorge. Rinse the okra, drain and cut into 1 cm (½ in.) slices.

Place the okra in a large bowl and add the tomato, onion, zucchini, potato, garlic, capsicum and parsley. Gently mix together. Pour the vegetables into a greased baking dish and then pour the olive oil and stock or water over the top. Season with salt and pepper. Bake in the oven for 1½ hours, until the vegetables are soft and tender. Set aside and keep warm.

Roast Beef Rump: Increase the oven temperature to 220°C (425°F/gas mark 7).

Rub the beef with the olive oil, oregano and pepper. Heat a large frying pan or skillet until quite hot. Add the beef and quickly brown on all sides to seal in the juices. Remove the meat from the pan and place in a baking dish. Roast in the oven for 30 minutes. Allow to rest for 15 minutes.

ROAST BEEF RUMP
1.5 kg (3 lb) piece of beef rump,
  trimmed of all fat
2 tablespoons virgin olive oil
1 teaspoon dried Greek
  (Mediterranean) oregano
freshly ground black pepper, to taste

TO SERVE
handful of kalamata olives, pitted
  and halved
60 g (2 oz) kefalotyri or pecorino
  cheese, shaved

Serves 6

To Serve: Mix the olives into the baked vegetables. Divide among 6 serving plates. Slice the beef into thin pieces and place several slices on top of each serving of vegetables. Top with some shavings of cheese and serve immediately.

PAN-ROASTED CHICKEN BREASTS WITH PICKLED FIGS AND ROAST GARLIC SKORDALIA

Kotopolo Stithos me Sika Toursi ke Skordalia

PICKLED FIGS

3 cups (750 mL/24 fl oz) white
    wine vinegar
2 cups (500 g/1 lb) sugar
1 teaspoon black peppercorns
10 whole cloves
10 whole allspice
4 bay leaves
1 stick cinnamon
1 teaspoon salt
1 clove garlic, unpeeled
1 kg (2 lb) black or green figs,
    washed and dried

ROAST GARLIC SKORDALIA

2 large waxy (boiling) potatoes,
    peeled and diced
6 heads of garlic, cloves peeled and
    rubbed with a little olive oil
salt and white pepper, to taste
juice of 1 lemon
½ cup (125 mL/4 fl oz) extra
    virgin olive oil

PAN-ROASTED CHICKEN BREASTS

6 boneless chicken breast fillets,
    with skin left on
olive oil, as needed
salt and freshly ground black
    pepper, to taste

Serves 6

THE COMBINATION OF chicken and figs is widely used throughout Greece, usually in a braise flavoured heavily with bay leaves. This refined version I created for my restaurant is delicious served with some creamy mashed potatoes or a plain rice pilaf.

Pickled Figs: Place all the ingredients except the figs in a stainless steel saucepan. Bring to the boil and simmer for 10 minutes. Add the figs and simmer for 1 minute. Pour the figs and pickling solution into a large preserving (canning) jar. Seal and store for at least 1 week before using.

Roast Garlic Skordalia: Preheat the oven to 120°C (250°F/gas mark ½ (S)).
   Boil the potatoes in a saucepan of salted water until tender. Drain. Meanwhile, bake the garlic cloves in the oven until tender, about 40 minutes. Remove the garlic cloves from the oven and increase the heat to 200°C (400°F/gas mark 6).
   Place the potato, garlic, salt, pepper and lemon juice in an electric blender or food processor. Process until well combined. With the motor still running, gradually add the olive oil and process until smooth. Set aside and keep warm.

Pan-roasted Chicken Breasts: Gently lift the skin off each of the chicken breasts to make a cavity or pocket. Place a sliced fig in each cavity. Season the chicken breast with salt and pepper, and brush with a little olive oil.
   Heat a large frying pan or skillet until quite hot. Add the chicken breasts and quickly brown on both sides. Place in a baking dish and roast in the oven for 8–10 minutes. Serve immediately with the Roast Garlic Skordalia.

VINE-ROASTED QUAIL STUFFED WITH RICE, CUMIN, PRESERVED LEMON AND PINE NUTS

Ortikia me Ambelofila Gemista

8 quails, boned and cleaned
extra virgin olive oil, as needed
rind of 1 lemon, grated
1 teaspoon fresh thyme leaves
freshly ground black pepper, to taste
16 vine (grape) leaves

STUFFING
1 small onion, finely chopped
1 clove garlic, finely chopped
¼ cup (60 mL/2 fl oz) virgin
*   olive oil*
½ teaspoon cumin seeds
½ cup (100 g/3 oz) long-grain rice
1 cup (250 mL/8 fl oz) chicken
*   stock*
salt, to taste
60 g (2 oz) pine nuts, lightly
*   toasted*
1 tablespoon finely chopped
*   preserved lemon (see page 111)*

SAUCE
500 g (1 lb) unripe or tart green
*   grapes, crushed in a blender*
*   and strained*
100 mL (3 fl oz) rich chicken stock
1 tablespoon fresh thyme leaves
1 cup (185 g/6 oz) sultana (small
*   white) grapes*

Serves 4-6

QUAILS ARE THE ONLY game birds available in Greece all year round. This is a great way to use them in autumn when fresh grape leaves are plentiful.

Place the quails or chicken, extra virgin olive oil, lemon rind, thyme and pepper in a bowl. Leave to marinate for at least 2 hours.

Stuffing: Sauté the onion and garlic in the olive oil over a medium heat until they are translucent. Add the cumin seeds and rice. Cook for 1 minute, stirring continuously. Now add the stock and salt. Simmer until the liquid has been absorbed. Remove from the heat and set aside. When cool, stir in the pine nuts and preserved lemon.

To Assemble the Dish: Preheat the oven to 200°C (400°F/gas mark 6).
    Lightly oil 6 sheets of aluminium foil (20 cm (8 in.) square). Place 2 vine leaves on top of each square. Make sure that they are slightly overlapping. Place a quail on top of each pair of vine leaves and fill generously with the stuffing. Fold the vine leaves over the quail and wrap with the foil to form a parcel.
    Place the quail parcels in a baking pan and roast in the oven for 10 minutes. Remove from the foil and roast for a further 15 minutes. Set the quails aside, keeping them warm and covered. Reserve the cooking juices for the sauce.

Sauce: Add the reserved cooking juices to a frying pan or skillet. Pour in the grape juice and reduce slightly over a moderate heat. Add the chicken stock and thyme, and continue to reduce the sauce until it thickens. Lastly, add the grapes and heat through for a few seconds. Serve accompanying the quail.

VEGETABLES

VEGETABLE DISHES HOLD a place of pride within Greek cuisine, mainly because of the Greek love of the land and what it can give back, but also historically because of poverty.

Perhaps another reason for the importance of vegetables in the Greek diet is the influence of the Greek Orthodox Church and its strict observance of Lent. Greeks had to abstain from food that derived from animals for forty days before Easter and Christmas, and also on Wednesdays and Fridays throughout the year if you were a good Christian.

At the height of the growing season, Greek vegetable markets, known as the *laiki agora* which literally translates as the 'people's market', are crammed with all kinds of wonderful vegetables, legumes and fruits — all waiting to be taken home and baked, stewed, puréed or stuffed.

But of all the vegetables available, none is held in as a great esteem as the bean. Beans of all types appear on the family table at least once a week. In summer, bean dishes are made from the fresh varieties available at the markets, while in winter many of the same dishes are made with dried beans. These dishes range from delicate purées enhanced with some garlic and simple salads dressed with some olive oil and lemon juice to slow-baked dishes spiked with tomatoes that make a substantial main course.

In all, the essence of Greek vegetable dishes is simplicity, allowing the vegetable to stand on its own and be appreciated and enjoyed for what it is.

BROCCOLI IN LEMON DRESSING

Brokoula me Latholemono

LEMON DRESSING
*100 mL (3 fl oz) extra virgin
    olive oil
rind of 2 lemons, peeled with a
    vegetable peeler and thinly
    sliced
juice of 1 lemon
salt and freshly ground black
    pepper, to taste*

BROCCOLI
*1 kg (2 lb) long-stemmed broccoli
    (rabe), stalks trimmed to 10 cm
    (4 in.) and peeled
1 lemon, cut into 6 wedges*

Serves 6

THE DRESSING IN THIS dish is used with almost all steamed green vegetables except, I've been told, amaranth. For this vegetable you use a dressing made with equal parts extra virgin olive oil and sweet white wine vinegar.

Lemon Dressing: Place all the dressing ingredients in a screw-top jar and shake vigorously. Set aside.

Broccoli: Steam the broccoli for 5 minutes, until tender.
    Shake the dressing and pour over the broccoli. Serve immediately, garnished with the lemon wedges.

ARTICHOKES BRAISED IN WHITE WINE AND ONIONS

Anginares me Krasi ke Kremidia

225 mL (7 fl oz) virgin olive oil
2 onions, finely chopped
500 g (1 lb) small pickling (boiling) onions, peeled and kept whole
9 globe artichokes, tough outer leaves removed, trimmed and halved, the stalks trimmed and peeled (keep in acidulated water*)
juice of 1 large lemon
salt and freshly ground black pepper, to taste
1 cup (250 mL/8 fl oz) light chicken stock or water
handful of fresh flat-leaf (Italian) parsley, finely chopped
handful of fresh dill, finely chopped

Serves 6

THIS IS A MUCH-FAVOURED DISH with many Greeks when globe artichokes are in season. This recipe was given to me by an aunt in Athens who used to run a taverna in her village.

Heat the olive oil in a large saucepan over a moderate heat. Add the onions and cook until they are translucent. Add the pickling onions and the artichoke halves, and cook for 5 minutes. Now add the lemon juice, salt, pepper and stock. Simmer for 30 minutes. Add the parsley and dill, and simmer for a further 5 minutes. Serve either hot or cold.

* *Acidulated water* is made by adding a small amount of vinegar, lemon juice or lime juice to water. It helps to prevent discoloration.

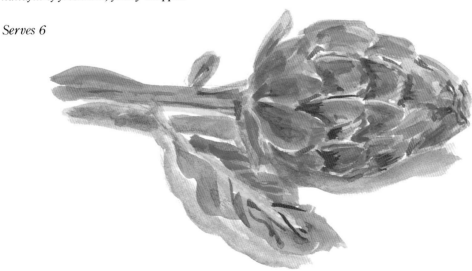

DEEP-FRIED ARTICHOKES STUFFED WITH FETA ON A BED OF BRIAM

Anginares Tiganites me Feta ke Briam

BRIAM

½ cup (125 mL/4 fl oz) virgin olive oil

2 brown (yellow) onions, finely chopped

3 cloves garlic, finely chopped

1 small chilli pepper, seeded and finely chopped

250 g (8 oz) eggplant (aubergine), cut into 1 cm (½ in.) cubes

250 g (8 oz) zucchini (courgette), cut into 1 cm (½ in.) cubes

250 g (8 oz) waxy (boiling) potatoes, cut into 1 cm (½ in.) cubes

1 large red capsicum (bell pepper), gently peeled with a potato peeler and cut into 1 cm (½ in.) cubes

500 g (1 lb) tomatoes, peeled, seeded and finely chopped

1 teaspoon dried oregano

1 small bunch of fresh flat-leaf (Italian) parsley, finely chopped

salt and freshly ground black pepper, to taste

1 tablespoon finely chopped fresh dill

BRIAM IS A BAKED VEGETABLE DISH and a favourite summer meal throughout Greece. I will always remember the time my maternal grandmother took me to meet her father who at the time was 100 years old. He was an amazing man who told me a lot about my ancestors and great stories about my grandmother when she was a child.

As we walked back to my grandmother's house that afternoon, an elderly woman walked by, holding a round baking dish from which came an ambrosial aroma. She was returning home from the bakery with the family lunch she had taken there that morning to be baked. It was a dish of *briam*, loaded with fantastic summer vegetables. Whenever I make *briam* myself, those smells and feelings always come rushing back. That was a great summer.

Briam: Preheat the oven to 180°C (350°F/ gas mark 4). Sauté the onions in 2 tablespoons of the olive oil until they are translucent. Add the garlic and chilli pepper, stir through and remove from the heat. Place the onion mixture, remaining vegetables, herbs and the remaining oil in a large bowl. Season with salt and pepper and spread into a baking dish. Bake in the oven for about 1 hour.

The *briam* can be served hot or at room temperature, so keep warm or allow to cool depending on your preference. Now prepare the artichokes.

ARTICHOKES

4 cups (1 L/1¾ imp. pts) extra
   virgin olive oil
12 small globe artichokes
juice of 1 lemon
300 g (10 oz) goat's milk or other
   feta cheese, mashed with a fork
plain (all-purpose) flour, seasoned
   with salt and freshly ground
   black pepper
sea salt, for sprinkling

Serves 6

Artichokes: Heat the oil to 180°C (350°F) in a deep-fryer or deep heavy saucepan.

Remove the tough outer leaves and cut away the tops of the artichokes. Trim the stalks to 5 cm (2 in.) from the base of the artichoke and peel the stalks. Open the artichokes carefully and remove some of the small centre leaves and choke. Fill the centre and within the larger leaves with the mashed feta and squeeze gently to form the original shape. Dip the artichokes in the seasoned flour to coat and shake off any excess flour.

Slip the artichokes, a few at a time, into the hot oil and fry until golden in colour, about 5 minutes. Drain on lots of paper towels or absorbent kitchen paper, and sprinkle with a little sea salt. Keep this process moving quickly as you need to serve the artichokes as soon as they are cooked.

Place a portion of *briam* onto each of 6 serving plates. Spread slightly so that it forms a bed on which the artichokes can sit. When all the artichokes are cooked, place 2 on each serving of briam. Serve immediately.

CAULIFLOWER FRITTERS

Kounoupidi Tiganito

1 large cauliflower, separated into
  small florets
¼ cup (60 mL/2 fl oz) white wine
  vinegar
small handful of fresh flat-leaf
  (Italian) parsley, finely chopped
1 teaspoon dried oregano
2 cups (250 g/8 oz) plain (all-
  purpose) flour
1 teaspoon baking powder
1 teaspoon salt
½ cup (125 mL/4 fl oz) milk
1 egg, beaten
¼ cup (60 g/2 oz) butter, melted
olive oil, for frying
lemon wedges, for serving

Serves 6

THROUGHOUT GREECE, CAULIFLOWERS — be they white or purple — are generally braised in white wine or with tomatoes, and are served either with lamb or as a meal on their own. This recipe, which I found in Crete, can also be made with broccoli.

Steam the cauliflower in a large saucepan for 10 minutes, until tender. Combine with the vinegar, parsley and oregano, and let stand for 15 minutes. Drain off the liquid.

Combine the flour, baking powder, salt, milk, egg and melted butter in a large bowl. Gently fold in the cauliflower.

Heat some olive oil in a large frying pan or skillet, enough to cover the bottom of the pan well. Place tablespoonfuls of the batter into the oil and fry until golden on both sides. Drain and serve hot with the lemon wedges.

NEW POTATOES GLAZED WITH RED WINE AND CORIANDER

Patates Spastes

RED WINE AND CORIANDER GLAZE
225 mL (7 fl oz) red wine
¼ cup (60 mL/2 fl oz) red wine
*   vinegar*
½ small onion, finely chopped
1 tablespoon coriander seeds,
*   crushed*
freshly ground black pepper, to taste

GARNISH
small handful of fresh flat-leaf
*   (Italian) parsley, coarsely*
*   chopped*
grated rind of 1 lemon
1 teaspoon capers, rinsed and
*   finely chopped (salt-preserved*
*   capers are best)*

NEW POTATOES
1 kg (2 lb) small new potatoes,
*   parboiled and halved*
vegetable oil, for deep-frying

Serves 6

THIS IS A CYPRIOT DISH, although traditionally the glaze would not be reduced and poured over the potatoes. Instead the potatoes are added to the glaze before it is reduced and the flavour allowed to permeate them. I find the potatoes too soft and mushy this way, but it's basically a question of taste.

Red Wine and Coriander Glaze: Place all the ingredients for the glaze in a small saucepan. Cook over a moderate heat until reduced to one-quarter of the original volume. Set aside.

Garnish: Combine all the garnish ingredients in a small bowl, cover and set aside.

New Potatoes: Preheat the oil in a deep-fryer to 180°C (250°F). Fry the potatoes until crisp and golden. Drain. Place the potatoes in a large bowl and pour the Red Wine and Coriander Glaze over them. Sprinkle with the garnish and serve immediately.

ROAST BANANA PEPPERS STUFFED WITH CHICKPEAS, SAFFRON AND PRESERVED LEMON

Piperies Yemistes

100 mL (3 fl oz) extra virgin
    olive oil
1 medium brown (yellow) onion,
    finely chopped
2 cloves garlic, finely chopped
1½ cups (250 g/8 oz) long-grain
    rice
250 g (8 oz) chickpeas, soaked
    overnight in cold water, rinsed
    and drained
3¼ cups (800 mL/26 fl oz)
    vegetable or chicken stock
½ teaspoon saffron threads
1 teaspoon dried oregano
⅓ cup (60 g/2 oz) currants
salt and freshly ground black
    pepper, to taste
12 red sweet banana or other
    peppers
½ preserved lemon slice, finely
    chopped (see page 111)
1 small bunch of fresh flat-leaf
    (Italian) parsley, finely chopped
¼ cup (60 mL/2 fl oz) extra virgin
    olive oil
100 mL (3 fl oz) dry white wine

ACCOMPANIMENT
deep-fried potatoes (see page 67)

Serves 6

SWEET BANANA PEPPERS are also known as Hungarian peppers, and come in different colours ranging from lime green and yellow to a bright red. They are quite sweet and are great stuffed and served as a main course with deep-fried potatoes.

Heat the olive oil in a saucepan over a moderate heat. Add the onion and garlic, and cook until they are translucent. Now add the rice and chickpeas, Cook for 2 minutes, stirring constantly.

Add the stock, saffron, oregano, currants and salt and pepper. Simmer until the liquid has been absorbed. Remove from the heat and allow to cool.

Preheat the oven to 190°C (375°F/gas mark 5).

Almost slice the top off each of the peppers, but leave partly attached so that this flap forms a 'lid' to reseal the pepper after stuffing. Carefully deseed.

Stir the preserved lemon and parsley into the stuffing mixture. Fill each of the peppers and seal with their 'lids'.

Place the peppers in a baking dish, pour over the olive oil and white wine, and roast for about 30 minutes, until lightly browned. Serve with the deep-fried potatoes.

GREEN PEAS WITH SPRING ONIONS

Arakas me Kremithakia

*2 bunches of small spring onions
    (scallions), peeled and trimmed
    to 1 cm (½ in.) of green stalk*
*½ cup (125 mL/4 fl oz) extra
    virgin olive oil*
*1.5 kg (3 lb) fresh green peas,
    shelled*
*small handful of fresh dill, finely
    chopped*
225 mL (7 fl oz) water
*salt and freshly ground black
    pepper, to taste*

Serves 6

THIS DISH IS DELICIOUS served either warm or cold.
It also makes the perfect accompaniment to grilled or
pan-fried lamb chops.

Add the spring onions and olive oil to a large
saucepan. Cook the spring onions over a low heat for
5–10 minutes, until lightly golden. Add the peas, dill
and water. Simmer for 15 minutes. Adjust the
seasoning to taste and serve either hot or cold.

GREEK-STYLE PRESERVED LEMONS

Lemonia Toursi

6 large lemons, washed well and dried
·6 tablespoons coarse sea salt
sprigs of dried oregano
bay leaves
whole cloves
virgin olive oil, to cover

Makes 1 large jar

AROUND THE ISLANDS OF the Dodecanese, some fruit from every lemon harvest is set aside for preserving. The lemons are lightly treated with salt and stored in olive oil, ready to be used in a multitude of dishes.

Cut the lemons into thick slices and remove any visible seeds. Place in a large bowl and sprinkle with the sea salt. Cover and refrigerate for 3 days, tossing well once every day.

Using a large preserving (canning) jar, layer the lemons with the herbs and cloves, and the juices that have developed during refrigeration. Cover with the olive oil and seal the jar. Store in a cool, dark place for at least 1 month before using.

GIANT BEANS BAKED WITH TOMATOES AND DILL

Gigantes me Tomates ke Anitho

*625 g (1¼ lb) large dried lima
(butter) beans, soaked overnight
in cold water, drained and
rinsed*

*225 mL (7 fl oz) extra virgin
olive oil*

3 onions, thinly sliced

2 carrots, peeled and finely chopped

1 stalk celery, finely chopped

4 cloves garlic, finely chopped

*500 g (1 lb) tomatoes, peeled,
seeded and finely chopped*

1 tablespoon dried oregano

1 teaspoon honey

*1 small bunch of fresh dill, finely
chopped*

*salt and freshly ground black
pepper, to taste*

Serves 6

THIS IS A POPULAR main course all over Greece
during Lent. The long, slow cooking in olive oil gives
this dish a sweet 'nutty' flavour and develops a sauce
which cries out to be mopped up with fresh, crusty
bread.

Place the lima beans in a saucepan. Cover well with
cold water and bring to the boil. Simmer for 1 hour.
Drain the beans, reserving ⅔ cup (150 mL/5 fl oz) of
the liquid.

Preheat the oven to 160°C (325°F/gas mark 3).

Heat the olive oil over a low heat in a large frying
pan or skillet. Sauté the onions, carrots and celery
for 20 minutes. Add the garlic, tomatoes, oregano,
honey, dill, beans, reserved liquid, salt and pepper.
Cook for a few minutes, stirring constantly.

Place the bean mixture in a baking dish and bake
for about 1½ hours, until the beans are tender and
most of the liquid has evaporated. Serve hot.

GREEK SALAD
Horiatiki

GREEK DRESSING

3 tablespoons extra virgin olive oil

1 tablespoon red wine vinegar

1 teaspoon dried Greek (Mediterranean) oregano

3 capers, finely chopped (salt-preserved capers are best)

1 tablespoon finely chopped fresh flat-leaf (Italian) parsley

freshly ground black pepper, to taste

GREEK SALAD

3 vine-ripened (sweet) egg (plum) tomatoes, cut into 6 pieces

1 cucumber, thinly sliced

½ red capsicum (bell pepper), seeded and thinly sliced

100 g (3 oz) feta cheese (preferably sheep's milk), diced

100 g (3 oz) kalamata olives

1 small red onion, thinly sliced (marinated for 2 hours in ¼ cup (60 mL/2 fl oz) red wine and ¼ cup (60 mL/2 fl oz) red wine vinegar)

Serves 4

MY MOTHER ONCE SAID the *bouzouki* was like sunshine for your ears, and enjoyed with a glass of retsina and *horiatiki*, nothing could be better.

Greek Dressing: Place all the dressing ingredients in a screw-top jar and shake vigorously. Set aside.

Greek Salad: Place the tomatoes in a large serving bowl. Layer the cucumber, capsicum, feta, olives and onion over the top.

Shake the dressing and pour over the salad. Serve.

BREADS AND PASTRIES

GREEKS LOVE BREAD and eat it at every meal. Whether it is a country-style bread or a sweet, highly decorated festive loaf, bread is always present on a Greek dinner table. In rural Greek villages, bread is still baked in the village *fournos*, a large dome-shaped oven fuelled by wood and used by the whole village.

To Greeks, bread is a sacred food. Making bread is considered a folk art, and home-baked bread is given as a gift and seen as an appreciation of good friendship.

Bread also has a place in Orthodox religion. Special breads are baked at Easter, Christmas and the New Year. The women of each congregation bake highly spiced breads for saints' days. These church breads are known as *artos*, the ancient word for bread. So crucial is bread to Greek culture that the word for cook in Greek, *mayeras*, is taken from the ancient word *maza*, which means 'that which is kneaded'.

Greeks also have a serious fondness for syrup-drenched pastries and biscuits (cookies), but they rarely end a meal with them. Instead, these are eaten between meals, usually with a cup of strong coffee and a long glass of iced water. Many of these pastries are baked for special festivals throughout the year. For instance, *kourambiethes* are baked for Easter and Christmas festivities, to be offered to family and friends who visit during these times.

COUNTRY-STYLE BREAD
Horiatiko Psomi

SOURDOUGH STARTER
*1½ cups (185 g/6 oz) bread
    (strong) flour*
1½ cups (375 mL/12 fl oz) water
½ teaspoon salt
1 teaspoon honey

BREAD
*½ cup (125 mL/4 fl oz) Sourdough
    Starter*
*1 cup (250 mL/8 fl oz) warm
    water*
*3¼ cups (400 g/13 oz) bread
    (strong) flour*
¾ cup (125 g/4 oz) cornmeal
1 teaspoon salt
2 tablespoons olive oil

Makes 1 loaf

HORIATIKO, AS THIS BREAD IS KNOWN, can be found in bakeries throughout Greece, with each region having its own variation. In Central Greece, where my family is from, it is made with a mixture of wholemeal (whole-wheat) flour and cornmeal, which happens to be my favourite version.

Sourdough Starter: Mix all the ingredients for the sourdough starter together well. Place in a covered container and leave to ferment at room temperature for 4–6 days before using.

Bread: The night before you bake this bread, mix the sourdough starter with the warm water and 1 cup (125 g/4 oz) of the flour in a large bowl. Cover and set aside in a warm place.

Place the bread flour, cornmeal and salt in a food processor. Whisk the oil into the starter mixture and, with the motor running, pour into the food processor. Process until it forms a ball of dough. Remove from the processor and knead on a lightly floured surface for at least 5 minutes. Place in an oiled bowl and set aside in a warm place to prove or rise for 2 hours.

Lightly oil a baking sheet and set aside. Knead the dough for another 5 minutes, shape into a round loaf and place on the baking sheet. Set aside in a warm place for 1 hour.

Preheat the oven to 180°C (350°F/gas mark 4). When the dough is ready, make several incisions on the surface of the loaf with a sharp knife. Bake in the oven for 35–40 minutes, until the crust is golden.

CHICKPEA BREAD

Eptosymo

2 cups (250 g/8 oz) chickpea flour
   (besan)
2 cups (500 mL/16 fl oz) hot water
large pinch of red pepper flakes
1 stick cinnamon
10 cups (1.25 kg/2 ½ lb) bread
   (strong) flour
½ cup (125 mL/4 fl oz) hot water
   (extra)
1 tablespoon salt
¼ cup (60 mL/2 fl oz) olive oil

Makes 2 loaves

THIS BREAD IS not so well known throughout Greece, and to date I have found it only in certain parts of Macedonia and Crete. It is quite rich in flavour and has a surprising kick which comes from the chilli added to the dough. It's delicious made into sandwiches layered with *pastourmas,* slices of boiled egg, *kefalotyri* or pecorino cheese and rocket (arugula).

Preheat the oven to the lowest possible setting (110°C/225°F/gas mark ¼ (S)). At the restaurant we use the oven with the pilot light on only.

Mix the chickpea flour, hot water, red pepper flakes and cinnamon stick together in a large bowl. Wrap the bowl in a cloth and leave in the oven overnight, with the door ajar. Remove from the oven and discard the cinnamon stick.

Place 2 cups (250 g/8 oz) of the bread flour into a bowl and stir in the chickpea mixture and extra hot water. Cover and set aside in a warm place for 2 hours. Place the remaining bread flour in another bowl. Stir in the salt, chickpea mixture and olive oil. Turn onto a floured surface and knead for 10 minutes. Divide into 2 round loaves and place on greased baking sheets. Set aside in a warm place for 1 hour. Preheat the oven to 180°C (350°F/gas mark 4).

When the dough is ready, place the loaves in the oven and bake for 50–60 minutes, until the crust is golden.

OREGANO FETA BREAD

Psomi me Rigani

225 mL (7 fl oz) warm water
30 g (1 oz) fresh (cake) yeast
100 mL (3 fl oz) olive oil
1 teaspoon salt
4 cups (500 g/1 lb) bread (strong)
flour
1 tablespoon dried Greek
(Mediterranean) oregano
1 small bunch of fresh oregano,
stems removed and leaves
chopped
250 g (8 oz) goat's milk or other
feta cheese, diced
olive oil (extra), as needed

Makes 1 loaf

GOAT'S MILK FETA works best in this bread. When cut into thick slices, brushed with olive oil and grilled, it's truly delicious.

Place the warm water in a bowl. Stir the yeast into it and set aside for about 10 minutes. Whisk in the olive oil and the salt.

Place the flour in a food processor and, with the motor running, pour in the yeasty liquid. Process the mixture until it forms a ball of dough.

Remove the dough and knead on a lightly floured surface for 5 minutes. Place the dough in a lightly oiled bowl and set aside in a warm place for 2 hours.

Now knead all the oregano and the feta into the dough. Shape into a round loaf and place on an oiled baking sheet. Set aside in a warm place for 1 hour.

Preheat the oven to 180°C (350°F/gas mark 4). When the dough is ready, cut a cross into the top of the loaf with a knife. Brush with the extra olive oil. Bake in the oven for 35–45 minutes, until the bottom of the loaf sounds hollow when tapped.

FENNEL BREAD

Marathopsomo

225 mL (7 fl oz) warm water
30 g (1 oz) fresh (cake) yeast
100 mL (3 fl oz) olive oil
1 teaspoon salt
2¾ cups (340 g/11 oz) bread
*   (strong) flour*
¾ cup (125 g/4 oz) fine semolina
1 heaped teaspoon fennel seeds
1 large onion, finely chopped and
*   sautéed in olive oil until golden*
sprinkling of semolina (extra)
olive oil (extra), as needed

Makes 1 loaf

I HAVE EATEN THIS BREAD in Greece twice, each time during a different season of the year. In winter it is made with the tender inner leaves of fennel bulbs, which give it a subtle fragrance. In summer, it is made with fennel seeds, giving it a more robust, earthier flavour. I love both versions, but at home I make the one with fennel seeds more often.

Place the warm water in a bowl. Stir in the yeast and set aside for about 10 minutes. Whisk in the olive oil and the salt. Set aside in a warm place.

Place the flour, semolina and fennel seeds in a food processor. With the motor running, pour in the yeasty liquid. Process the mixture until it gathers into a ball of dough.

Remove the dough and knead on a lightly floured surface for 5 minutes. Form into a ball shape and place in a lightly oiled bowl. Cover and set aside in a warm place for 2 hours.

Now take the dough and knead in the onions. Shape into a long loaf and place on an oiled baking sheet. Sprinkle with the extra semolina and set aside in a warm place for 1 hour.

Preheat the oven to 180°C (350°F/gas mark 4). Brush the top of the loaf with olive oil and bake in the oven for 35–45 minutes, until the bottom of the loaf sounds hollow when tapped.

TSOUREKI

Tsoureki

SPICED LIQUID
1 scant teaspoon whole cloves
10 whole allspice
10 black peppercorns
1 stick cinnamon
3 fresh bay leaves
¼ cup (60 mL/2 fl oz) brandy
½ cup (125 mL/4 fl oz) water

YEAST MIXTURE
1½ cups (375 mL/12 fl oz) milk,
*   scalded and kept warm*
2 envelopes active dry yeast
1 cup (125 g/4 oz) plain (all-
*   purpose) flour, sifted*
2 tablespoons light honey

DOUGH
7 cups (875 g/28 oz) plain (all-
*   purpose) flour, sifted*
½ teaspoon salt
¾ cup (185 g/6 oz) caster
*   (superfine) sugar*
rind of 1 orange, finely grated,
*   dried in a slow oven with*
*   2 tablespoons caster (superfine)*
*   sugar and ground*
125 g (4 oz) unsalted butter, cut
*   into small pieces and kept cold*
4 eggs, beaten until thick and
*   creamy*
1 egg yolk (extra), lightly beaten

Makes 2 loaves

TSOUREKI IS A FESTIVE BREAD that is traditionally baked during Easter. The red eggs that normally decorate it are supposed to symbolise the blood of Christ, as well as eternity and fertility. *Tsoureki* has a texture similar to brioche. At Cosmos, we grill thick slices of it, which are then topped with wedges of very slowly poached nectarines and thick cream, and served as a simple but delicious dessert.

Spiced Liquid: Bring all the ingredients to the boil in a small saucepan. Simmer, covered, for 15 minutes. Remove from the heat and set aside to cool, still keeping covered.

Yeast Mixture: Stir the milk, yeast, flour and honey together in a large bowl. Cover and set aside in a warm place for about 1 hour.

Dough: Stir the flour, salt, sugar and orange rind together in a large bowl. Add the butter and use your fingertips to rub into the flour mixture. Make a well in the centre. Strain the spiced liquid and add it, the yeast mixture and the beaten eggs (minus the extra egg yolk) to the flour mixture. Stir until a dough begins to form. Adjust the consistency with more milk or flour if necessary. The dough should be smooth.

Turn out onto a lightly floured surface and knead for 10 minutes. Place in a greased bowl and set aside in a warm place for about 2 hours.

Punch down (knock back) the dough. Divide into two and knead each ball of dough for another 5 minutes. Shape into 2 round loaves. Set aside in a warm place for another 2 hours.

Preheat the oven to 180°C (350°F/gas mark 4). When the dough is ready, brush the tops of the loaves with the extra egg yolk and bake in the oven for 45 minutes, until their crusts are golden.

WHITE SHORTBREAD CRESCENTS

Kourambiethes

*250 g (8 oz) unsalted butter, at
   room temperature*
*⅔ cup (100 g/3 oz) icing
   (confectioners') sugar, sifted*
1 teaspoon vanilla extract (essence)
2 egg whites
1 tablespoon ouzo (optional)
*4 cups (500 g/1 lb) plain (all-
   purpose) flour*
1 teaspoon baking powder
*¾ cup (100 g/3 oz) almond slivers,
   toasted*
¼ cup (60 mL/2 fl oz) rose-water
*1¼ cups (225 g/7 oz) icing
   (confectioners') sugar (extra),
   sifted*

Makes 36

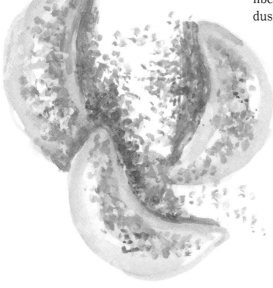

KOURAMBIETHES, AS THESE BISCUITS (COOKIES) are known to Greeks, must be the most popular sweet treat in the country. They appear at weddings, birthdays, namedays, christenings and every other holiday throughout the country. At Cosmos, we serve them occasionally with coffee, and to date I have never seen a plate of these biscuits come back to the kitchen with any left on it.

Preheat the oven to 160°C (325°F/gas mark 3). Grease two baking sheets and set aside.

Beat the butter in an electric mixer for at least 10 minutes, until very light and creamy. Add the icing sugar, vanilla, egg whites and ouzo, and beat until smooth.

Sift the flour and baking powder together into the butter mixture and fold through until well combined. Fold in the almond slivers.

Break off pieces of dough the size of a walnut and shape into crescents. Place on the baking sheets and bake in the oven for 15 minutes, until golden. Remove from the oven, sprinkle with rose-water and dust liberally with the extra icing sugar. Allow to cool and dust again with icing sugar.

ANISEED AND SESAME STICKS

Koulourakia me Glikaniso ke Sousami

½ cup (125 mL/4 fl oz) olive oil
1 teaspoon aniseed
2 tablespoons sesame seeds
½ cup (125 g/4 oz) caster
    (superfine) sugar
⅓ cup (90 mL/3 fl oz) orange juice
finely grated rind of 1 orange
5 cups (625 g/1¼ lb) plain (all-
    purpose) flour
1 teaspoon ground cinnamon

Makes approximately 24

THIS STYLE OF biscuit (cookie) is eaten throughout Greece during Lent as it has no dairy products in it — usually dipped into a cup of morning coffee. They are also delicious dipped into a glass of fortified muscat or served with thick cream.

Preheat the oven to 180°C (350°F/gas mark 4). Lightly oil two baking sheets and set aside.

In a small saucepan, heat the olive oil, aniseed and sesame seeds over a low heat for 5 minutes. Cool slightly and add the sugar, orange juice and orange rind.

Sift the flour and cinnamon into a large mixing bowl. Make a well in the centre and add the oil mixture. Gradually combine these ingredients and then work the dough with your hands until it is smooth. Cover with plastic wrap (cling film) and chill for 30 minutes.

Take a piece of dough the size of a whole walnut and roll into a thin rope shape about 20 cm (8 in.) long. Repeat this process with the remaining dough and place the fingers of dough on the baking sheets in rows, allowing enough space in between for the biscuits to spread. Bake in the oven for 15 minutes, until golden in colour.

QUINCE MERINGUE WRAPPED IN FILO PASTRY

Kithoni Marenga Rollo me Filo

SYRUP
1⅓ cups (350 g/11 oz) sugar
1 cup (250 mL/8 fl oz) water
juice of ½ lemon

MERINGUE FILLING
6 eggs, separated
1½ cups (250 g/8 oz) icing
(confectioners') sugar
4½ cups (500 g/1 lb) almond meal
(ground almonds)
250 g (8 oz) poached quinces,
drained and chopped (see
page 137)
1 teaspoon vanilla essence (extract)

PASTRY
500 g (1 lb) filo pastry
¾ cup (185 g/6 oz) unsalted
butter, melted

Makes 36

THIS IS A VERY RICH pastry which is ideal sliced thinly and served with coffee.

Syrup: Combine all the ingredients in a saucepan. Bring to the boil and simmer for 15 minutes. Set aside to cool.

Meringue Filling: Beat the egg yolks with the sugar until thick and creamy. In a separate bowl, beat the egg whites until stiff peaks form. Fold the ground almonds, quinces and vanilla essence into the egg yolk mixture. Gently fold in the egg whites.

To Assemble the Pastry: Preheat the oven to 150°C (300°F/gas mark 2).

Divide the filo pastry into 4 portions lengthways. Take one portion of filo and brush each sheet with the melted butter, laying one on top of the other. Keep the unprepared filo covered with a damp cloth.

Take one prepared portion of filo and spread a quarter of the meringue filling at the base of the length of pastry. Gently roll the filo up, folding in the edges so the filling doesn't ooze out. Repeat this process with the 3 remaining portions of filo.

Place the rolls on a baking sheet. Brush with melted butter and bake for about 1 hour, until golden in colour. Remove from the oven and slowly pour the syrup over the pastries. When ready to serve, cut into thin slices.

DESSERTS

THERE IS NO DOUBT that most Greeks have a sweet tooth, but what follows a meal, even in restaurants, is usually a luscious piece of fresh seasonal fruit, whether it be figs and grapes in autumn, or peaches and watermelon in summer.

What we would normally call desserts are eaten as a separate meal in Greece. Most times these are consumed at the local *zaharoplastio* or pastry shop. Here many Greeks meet friends and family either during the day or late in the evening for coffee and sweet treats. The skills necessary to be a *zaharoplastis* (sugar sculptor) elevate cake and pastry making to a fine art. There is a breathtakingly enormous range of Greek desserts, cakes and pastries, which fall into several categories.

There are *glyka tou tapsiou*, 'sweets from the baking dish', which are cakes or filo pastries such as baklava, sticky walnut cake and *galaktoboureko*. These are the baked sweet treats that are drenched in honey or sugar syrup, and they are often perfumed with orange blossom or rich spices.

Then there are *glyka tou koutaliou*, 'spoon sweets', which are sweetmeats that are made between spring and early autumn. Almost any fruit or vegetable is preserved for these, with some of the most popular being sour cherries, orange peel, quince and eggplant (aubergine). Evenly highly perfumed spring roses are cultivated with a view to making a delicate rose-petal preserve.

There are also the very popular fried pastries. These range from *diples* and *xerotiganites*, to *loukoumades* or batter fritters, all of which are doused with a sticky honey syrup and sprinkled with cinnamon, crushed nuts or sesame seeds.

Finally, there are the puddings or desserts, most of which are made and served in individual bowls, to be eaten by whomever, whenever. These include rice puddings, halva and *moustalevria* or grape must pudding.

CARAMELISED SUGAR PUDDING WITH PERSIMMON AND FRESH MINT

Halva Farsalon

*2½ cups (625 mL/1 imp. pt) warm
    water*
*2 cups (250 g/8 oz) rice flour
    (available in good delicatessens
    and health food stores)*
1⅓ cups (300 g/10 oz) white sugar
*1 cup (150 g/5 oz) soft brown
    sugar*
90 g (3 oz) unsalted butter
*¾ cup (100 g/3 oz) almond slivers,
    lightly toasted*
3 ripe persimmons, sliced
*small handful of fresh mint leaves,
    finely shredded*

Serves 6

THIS PUDDING IS known as *halva farsalon* in Greece. It comes from Farsala in Thessaly, and trays of it can be found in almost every bakery in the northern regions of Greece. At the restaurant we serve it in glass bowls, chilled and topped with thick slices of ripe persimmon and a sprinkling of finely shredded mint leaves.

Put the warm water into a bowl. Whisk the rice flour into the water and keep warm over a saucepan of hot water.

Put ⅓ cup (90 g/3 oz) of the white sugar in a large, heavy cast-iron or enamel saucepan. Heat over a medium heat until it caramelises, stirring continuously so it does not burn.

Add the rice flour and water, the remaining white sugar, brown sugar, butter and almonds. Reduce the heat to very low. Beat the mixture continuously with a wooden spoon, as you would when making polenta. Continue cooking until the spoon can almost stand upright in the pudding.

Remove from the heat and divide among 6 serving bowls. Cover the bowls with plastic wrap (cling film) and chill for at least 2 hours before serving. Serve topped with the persimmon slices and a sprinkling of mint.

MEDITERRANEAN NUT TART WITH ANISEED CUSTARD

Karidopitta me Glikaniso Crema

ANISEED CUSTARD

6 egg yolks
½ cup (125 g/4 oz) sugar
300 mL (10 fl oz) milk
300 mL (10 fl oz) thickened
    (heavy, double) cream
30 g (1 oz) aniseed, lightly crushed
1 vanilla bean (pod), cut in half
    lengthwise

MEDITERRANEAN NUT TART

6 sheets thick filo pastry
butter, melted
150 mL (5 fl oz) thickened (heavy,
    double) cream
60 g (2 oz) butter
¼ cup (100 g/3 oz) honey
½ cup (100 g/3 oz) soft brown
    sugar
½ teaspoon aniseed, crushed
2 cups (225 g/7 oz) almond flakes
    (sliced almonds)
½ cup (150 g/5 oz) chopped
    walnuts
100 g (3 oz) pine nuts
100 g (3 oz) dried figs, softened in
    ¼ cup (60 mL/2 fl oz) brandy
    and chopped

Serves 8

THIS TART IS VERY LIKE the traditional nut-filled filo sweets so familiar in Greek cuisine. It is not, however, drenched in a sugar syrup, but rather served with a subtle, anise-flavoured custard.

Aniseed Custard: Beat the egg yolks and sugar together until pale and creamy. Put the milk, cream and aniseed in a saucepan. Scrape the seeds out of the vanilla bean into the saucepan. Bring the mixture just to the boil, then let it cool slightly. Stir into the egg mixture.

Pour into a clean saucepan and stir over a moderate heat until the custard coats the back of a spoon. Let the custard cool and strain out the aniseed and vanilla seeds. Cover the custard and chill in the refrigerator until needed.

Mediterranean Nut Tart: Preheat the oven to 180°C (350°F/gas mark 4). Grease a 25 cm (10 in.) tart pan with removable base. Brush the sheets of filo pastry with the melted butter. Line the pan with the filo and trim the edges of the pastry. Set aside.

Bring the cream, butter, honey, brown sugar and aniseed to the boil in a saucepan. Reduce the heat to low. Simmer for 10 minutes. Stir in the nuts and figs. Spread over the filo pastry and smooth the surface.

Bake in the oven for 35 minutes, until golden brown. Cool and serve with the Aniseed Custard.

COCONUT CUSTARD TART WITH POACHED QUINCES

Galaktoboureko me Karida ke Kidonia

6 sheets thick filo pastry
unsalted butter, melted
1 vanilla bean (pod), split
*   lengthwise*
3 cups (750 mL/24 fl oz) milk
90 g (3 oz) coconut milk powder
⅓ cup (60 g/2 oz) fine semolina
¾ cup (185 g/6 oz) caster
*   (superfine) sugar*
125 g (4 oz) unsalted butter, cut
*   into small pieces*
3 eggs, lightly beaten
4 quinces, poached (see page 137)

Serves 8

GALAKTOBOUREKO IS A RICH CUSTARD SLICE and is one of my favourite desserts. However, it is far too sweet for most people, so I have adapted a recipe my mother gave me and made it into a coconut-flavoured tart. It is topped with thick slices of poached quince and served with some of the poaching syrup around each slice.

Preheat the oven to 160°C (325°F/gas mark 3). Grease a 23 cm (9 in.) tart pan with removable base. Line the pan with the filo pastry, brushing each sheet liberally with the melted butter. Trim the edges of the pastry and cover with a damp cloth. Set aside.

Scrape the seeds out of the vanilla bean. Place the milk, coconut powder and vanilla seeds in a large saucepan. Bring to the boil. Stir well, then reduce the heat to low. Mix the semolina and the sugar together in a small bowl. Sprinkle into the milk mixture, whisking constantly. Simmer for 6–7 minutes, still whisking constantly. Remove from the heat and beat in the pieces of butter, then the eggs. Beat until well incorporated.

Remove the cloth from the tart case and pour the custard into it. Bake for about 50 minutes, until set firm. Remove from the oven and cover the top of the tart with thick slices of poached quince. Drizzle some of the poaching syrup over the top. Place the tart in the oven for a further 15 minutes. Cool before serving.

WARM ORANGE AND ALMOND CAKE WITH SPICED ORANGES

Amiglalopitta me Portakalia

SPICED ORANGES

8 oranges, peeled and cut into
segments with all the white pith
removed (keep all the juices to
add to the syrup)
⅔ cup (150 g/5 oz) sugar
2 cups (500 mL/16 fl oz)
mavrodaphne *or other sweet*
red wine
1 bay leaf
6 whole cloves
1 stick cinnamon

ORANGE AND ALMOND CAKE

1 cup (225 g/7 oz) caster
(superfine) sugar
5 eggs, separated
250 g (8 oz) unsalted butter,
melted
½ cup (125 mL/4 fl oz) fresh
orange juice
grated rind of 2 oranges
1¾ cups (225 g/7 oz) plain (all-
purpose flour, sifted with 1
tablespoon baking powder
2 cups (225 g/7 oz) almond meal
(ground almonds)

TO SERVE

thickened (heavy, double) cream,
whipped

Serves 8

ORANGES AND ALMONDS ARE widely used in cakes throughout Greece. This recipe is similar to *pantespani*, a sponge cake, and I love to serve it warm with a syrupy citrus salad and lashings of thick cream.

Spiced Oranges: Cover the orange segments and chill until required. Heat the sugar, wine, spices and orange juices from the segments in a saucepan. Bring to the boil and simmer for 10 minutes, until the syrup thickens. Cool the syrup and pour over the orange segments. Chill for at least 2 hours.

Orange and Almond Cake: Preheat the oven to 190°C (375°F/gas mark 5). Grease a 23 cm (9 in.) round cake pan. Set aside.

Beat the sugar and egg yolks together in a bowl, until pale and creamy. Stir in the melted butter, orange juice, rind, sifted flour and almond meal. Beat the egg whites until soft peaks form. Carefully fold into the batter. Pour the batter into the cake pan and bake for 10 minutes. Lower the oven temperature to 180°C (350°F/gas mark 4) and bake for another 30 minutes. Allow the cake to cool in the pan for 10 minutes.

Serve the cake accompanied by the Spiced Oranges and whipped cream.

FROZEN CHOCOLATE TOURTA WITH ORANGE BLOSSOM SYRUP

Tourta Tou Psigio me Anthonero Siropi

FROZEN CHOCOLATE TOURTA

500 g (1 lb) dark (semisweet) chocolate

1 tablespoon Greek-style coffee

1 tablespoon cognac

100 mL (3 fl oz) thickened (heavy, double) cream

225 g (7 oz) butter, at room temperature

1¼ cups (225 g/7 oz) icing (confectioners') sugar

3 eggs, separated

¾ cup (100 g/3 oz) almond slivers, toasted

⅔ cup (100 g/3 oz) candied orange peel

ORANGE BLOSSOM SYRUP

1 cup (250 g/8 oz) sugar

1 cup (250 mL/8 fl oz) water

1 tablespoon orange blossom water

Serves 8-10

THIS *TOURTA* IS TRADITIONALLY layered with sponge fingers soaked in cognac before freezing, then served at room temperature covered in whipped cream.

Frozen Chocolate Tourta: Grease a 4-cup (1 L/ 1¾ imp. pt.) loaf pan and line with greaseproof (waxed) paper. Set aside.

In a double boiler, melt the chocolate with the coffee, cognac and cream. Mix well and set aside to cool. Beat the butter and icing sugar together in a bowl, until creamy. Beat the egg yolks in one at a time. Stir the chocolate mixture, almonds and orange peel into butter mixture.

Whisk the egg whites until they form soft peaks. Gently fold in the chocolate mixture. Pour into the loaf pan. Freeze for at least 4 hours. While the *tourta* is freezing, prepare the Orange Blossom Syrup.

Orange Blossom Syrup: Bring the sugar and water to the boil in a saucepan. Simmer for 5 minutes. Add the orange blossom water and leave to cool. Chill the syrup until ready to use.

To Serve: Carefully remove the *tourta* from the loaf pan. Slice and serve immediately, with some of the syrup drizzled over each slice.

DIPLES WITH PASSIONFRUIT CREAM AND MANGO

Diples me Krema ke Frouta

ELENI'S DIPLES PASTRY
1¼ cups (150 g/5 oz) plain (all-
 purpose) flour
2 teaspoons baking powder
pinch of salt
2 eggs
30 mL (1 fl oz) olive oil
grated rind of 1 orange
1 tablespoon brandy or ouzo
vegetable oil, for deep-frying

PASSIONFRUIT CREAM
1 cup (250 mL/8 fl oz) thickened
 (heavy, double) cream
1 tablespoon icing (confectioners')
 sugar
pulp of 6 passionfruit
2 mangoes, peeled and sliced
icing (confectioners') sugar (extra),
 for dusting

Serves 8

DIPLES ARE CRISP, FRIED PASTRIES made all over Greece. They come in many different shapes — bows, knots, rolls, plain strips and even intricate flower buds. *Diples* are almost always served drenched in a honey syrup and sprinkled with crushed nuts and/or sesame seeds. At Cosmos, we serve them almost as a casing (crust), layered with different cream and fruit fillings. This filling is extremely popular and it's very easy to make. Strawberries can be used instead of mangoes if you find these hard to buy.

Eleni's Diples Pastry: Mix the flour, baking powder and salt together in a food processor. In a small bowl, lightly whisk the eggs, olive oil, orange rind and brandy or ouzo. With the motor running, slowly pour this mixture into the food processor and process until it forms a ball. Remove the dough and wrap in plastic wrap (cling film). Refrigerate for 1 hour.

Divide the dough into four pieces. Taking one piece at a time, roll the dough out on a floured board until it is paper thin. Cut into 8 cm x 8 cm (3 in. x 3 in.) squares, making approximately 16 squares in all.

In a deep-fryer, heat the oil to 180°C (350°F). Drop the squares, one at a time, into the oil. When they rise to the surface, turn them over. Fry until they turn a light golden colour, about 1–2 minutes. Drain the *diples* on lots of paper towels or absorbent kitchen paper. Leave to cool.

Passionfruit Cream: Whisk the cream with the icing sugar until stiff. Fold the passionfruit pulp through the cream. Pipe the cream onto a *diples*, top with a few mango slices and a little more cream. Sandwich together with another *diples*. Dust the top with the extra icing sugar.

PEARS BAKED IN MUSCAT WITH PISTACHIOS

Ahladia Sto Fourno me Moscato ke Foundouckia

6 firm but ripe pears
juice of 1 lemon
100 g (3 oz) shelled unsalted
   pistachio nuts, chopped
75 g (2½ oz) caster (superfine)
   sugar
finely grated rind of 1 orange
100 g (3 oz) unsalted butter, at
   room temperature
1 cup (250 mL/8 fl oz) Samos or
   other muscat wine
thickened (heavy, double) cream,
   lightly whipped, or honey
   yoghurt, to serve

Serves 6

CHOOSE FIRM, FRAGRANT PEARS for this autumn dish. At the restaurant, I use the beurre bosc, a small, brown, beautifully-shaped pear which cooks very well.

Preheat the oven to 180°C (350°F/gas mark 4).
   Peel, halve and core the pears, leaving the stems intact. Sprinkle with lemon juice.
   Combine the pistachios, caster sugar, orange rind and butter to make a paste. Place the pear halves in a baking dish and mound the paste in the cored centre of each one. Pour the muscat into the bottom of the dish.
   Bake in the oven for about 25 minutes, basting occasionally with the wine. Serve hot, topped with the cream or honey yoghurt.

PEARS WITH HONEY AND KEFALOTYRI

Ahladia me Meli ke Kefalotiri

6 medium, almost-ripe pears
6 tablespoons light honey
thick shavings of kefalotyri *or*
    mild Parmesan cheese
freshly ground white pepper, to
    taste

Serves 6

THIS SIMPLE BUT DELICIOUS recipe was given to me by an aunt in Athens who declared it one of the best ways to eat pears. I love this recipe, too, and at the restaurant we serve it with a honey yoghurt ice cream and some lightly toasted walnuts.

Preheat the grill (broiler).

Peel, halve and core the pears, leaving the stems intact. Score the uncut side of each pear half and place on a baking tray cut side down. Pour half a tablespoon of honey over each pear half, then top with a few shavings of *kefalotyri* or Parmesan, and a sprinkling of white pepper.

Place under the grill until the pears are lightly browned and the cheese has melted. Serve the pears immediately either on their own or with ice cream or frozen yoghurt.

COS LEMON AND HONEY TART WITH BURNT HONEY CUSTARD

Lemonopitta Apo Tin ke me Limoni ke Meli

CANDIED LEMONS
6 lemons
4 cups (1 kg/2 lb) white sugar
4 cups (1 L/1¾ imp. pts) water
1 vanilla bean (pod), split
    lengthwise
1 sprig lemon-scented geranium or
    lemon verbena

PASTRY
2 cups (250 g/8 oz) plain (all-
    purpose) flour
⅓ cup (60 g/2 oz) icing
    (confectioners') sugar
125 g (4 oz) unsalted butter,
    chilled and cut into small pieces
30 mL (1 fl oz) plain yoghurt
2 egg yolks

FILLING
100 g (3 oz) unsalted butter, at
    room temperature
¼ cup (100 g/3 oz) honey
7 egg yolks
1⅓ cups (150 g/5 oz) almond meal
    (ground almonds)
⅓ cup (90 mL/3 fl oz) lemon juice
150 mL (5 fl oz) thickened (heavy,
    double) cream
¾ cup (185 mL/6 fl oz) Candied
    Lemons, drained

BURNT HONEY CUSTARD
⅓ cup (125 g/4 oz) honey
2½ cups (625 mL/1 imp. pt) milk
6 egg yolks

Serves 6-8

A TRADITIONAL VERSION of this tart would be baked without the candied lemon, but drenched instead in a sticky lemon syrup. Although it is delicious that way, this adaptation is equally so.

This tart is a speciality from the island of Cos and to this day I haven't found another region in Greece that makes this style of tart.

Candied Lemons: Cut the lemons in half lengthways and slice thinly, removing all the pips (seeds) as you go. Put the slices in a bowl and pour boiling water over them to cover. Let stand for 1 hour. Drain and rinse the lemons. Cover them with boiling water once more and let stand for another hour.

Now drain the lemons and rinse with cold water. Bring the sugar, water and vanilla bean slowly to the boil in a large saucepan. Add the lemon slices and lemon geranium or verbena, reduce the heat and simmer gently for about 2 hours, until the syrup has reduced and taken on a golden tinge. Remove from the heat and take out the vanilla bean and lemon geranium or verbena. Store the syrup in the refrigerator. Do not remove the lemon slices.

Pastry: Place the flour and icing sugar in a food processor. Process to mix thoroughly. Add the butter and process for only a few seconds, just long enough to incorporate the butter. Lightly beat the yoghurt and egg yolks together in a small bowl. With the motor running, add this mixture and process until it forms a ball. Remove the dough from the processor and cover with plastic wrap (cling film). Refrigerate for 1 hour.

Preheat the oven to 190°C (375°F/gas mark 5).

Roll out the pastry to fit a 23 cm (9 in.) tart pan with a removable base. Bake blind in the oven for 8 minutes (that is, without filling, the pastry having been pricked with a fork, lined with silicon paper (baking parchment) and filled with rice, dried beans or ceramic pie weights). Remove from the oven and set aside. Reduce the oven temperature to 180°C (350°F/gas mark 4).

Filling: Beat the butter and honey together in a bowl, until pale and creamy. Add the egg yolks, almond meal and lemon juice. Mix until well combined. Gently fold in the cream. Spoon the candied lemons onto the bottom of the prepared tart case (shell). Gently pour over the filling. Bake in the oven for 30 minutes. Serve the tart cold, sliced into wedges and accompanied by the Burnt Honey Custard.

Burnt Honey Custard: Bring the honey to the boil in a small saucepan. Simmer gently for 3–4 minutes. Set aside. Heat the milk to just below boiling in another saucepan and set aside.

Beat the egg yolks until pale and creamy. Pour the honey over them and continue beating until thoroughly mixed. Now slowly pour in the milk, stirring constantly.

Return the custard to a clean saucepan and stir over a moderate heat until the custard coats the back of a spoon. Cool, strain the custard into a container, cover and chill until ready to serve.

STICKY YOGHURT CAKE WITH RAISIN SYRUP

Yiaourtopita me Stafida

RAISIN SYRUP
1½ cups (250 g/8 oz) raisins
100 mL (3 fl oz) brandy
30 mL (1 fl oz) ouzo
90 mL (3 fl oz) lemon juice
475 mL (15 fl oz) water
1 cup (250 g/8 oz) sugar

STICKY YOGHURT CAKE
4 eggs, separated
⅓ cup (100 g/3 oz) caster
*   (superfine) sugar*
¼ cup (100 g/3 oz) light honey
280 g (9 oz) plain (all-purpose)
*   flour*
1 tablespoon baking powder
pinch of salt
finely grated rind of 2 lemons
90 g (3 oz) unsalted butter, melted
*   and cooled*
400 mL (13 fl oz) Greek-style
*   yoghurt*

Serves 8

THIS STYLE OF CAKE has played a role in many family celebrations in many homes in Greece. Traditionally, it is served with lots of sticky lemon syrup, the type that only a cup of good Greek coffee could counteract.

Raisin Syrup: Soak the raisins in the brandy and ouzo, preferably overnight. In a pan, heat the raisins and their syrup with the lemon juice, water and sugar. Bring to the boil and simmer for 15 minutes. Set aside to cool.

Sticky Yoghurt Cake: Preheat the oven to 180°C (350°F/gas mark 4). Grease and flour a 23 cm (9 in.) cake pan.

Beat the egg yolks with the caster sugar and honey until pale and creamy. Sift the flour, baking powder and salt together into a large bowl. Stir in the egg mixture and the lemon rind. Now stir in the melted butter and yoghurt, and incorporate well.

Whisk the egg whites until they form stiff peaks. Stir one-third into the cake batter to lighten. Gently fold in the remaining egg whites and pour the batter into the cake pan. Bake for about 35 minutes. Pour some of the raisin syrup over the cake and allow to soak through the cake. Serve the slices of cake with the poached raisins and more of the syrup.

POACHED QUINCES WITH RICE PUDDING

Kithoni se Siropi me Rizogalo

POACHED QUINCES

2 cups (500 g/16 oz) sugar

2 cups (500 mL/16 fl oz)
   mavrodaphne or other sweet
   red wine

1 cup (250 mL/8 fl oz) water

1 bay leaf

6 whole cloves

6 whole allspice

1 stick cinnamon, crumbled

6 quinces, peeled, cored and
   quartered (Keep in acidulated
   water, i.e. immersed in water
   with a small amount of vinegar,
   lemon juice or lime juice added
   to it. This prevents
   discoloration.)

RICE PUDDING

½ cup (100 g/3 oz) arborio or
   other short-grain rice

3¼ cups (800 mL/26 fl oz) milk

75 g (2½ oz) caster (superfine)
   sugar

30 g (1 oz) butter

pinch of salt

1 vanilla bean (pod), cut in half
   lengthwise

2 egg yolks

¼ cup (60 mL/2 fl oz) thickened
   (heavy, double) cream

½ teaspoon rose-water

Serves 6

IN GREEK MYTHOLOGY, it was believed that the quince was the 'golden apple' that Paris awarded to Aphrodite when he made the ill-fated judgment that sparked off the Trojan wars. It became her fruit — the fruit of love, marriage and fertility.

I have been told that the best quinces in the world come from Kydonia in Crete, hence the Greek name for quince, *kythoni*.

Poached Quinces: Bring the sugar, wine, water and spices to the boil in a saucepan. Drain the quinces and add to this syrup. Reduce the heat and simmer for at least 3 hours. Serve warm or cold with the Rice Pudding.

Rice Pudding: Place the rice, milk, caster sugar, butter and salt into a heavy saucepan. Scrape the seeds out of the vanilla bean into the saucepan. Bring to the boil, then cover and simmer for about 1 hour, stirring occasionally, until the mixture is very thick and creamy. Do not remove from the heat.

In a small bowl, whisk the egg yolks, cream and rose-water until thoroughly mixed. Stir into the rice mixture and cook for 1 minute. Divide the mixture among 6 lightly oiled dariole or small jelly moulds. Chill for several hours. Unmould and serve with the poached quinces, pouring some of the syrup over the pudding.

CHOCOLATE FIG BAKLAVA

Baklava me Tsokalata ke Sika

FILO PASTRY
125 g (4 oz) dark (semisweet)
chocolate
8 cups (1 kg/2 lb) plain (all-
purpose) flour
½ teaspoon salt
100 g (3 oz) butter, placed in the
freezer for at least 2 hours
1 egg
1 cup (250 mL/8 fl oz) sparkling
mineral water

CHOCOLATE FIG FILLING
4 cups (500 g/1 lb) chopped
walnuts
4 cups (500 g/1 lb) chopped
almonds
350 g (11 oz) breadcrumbs (made
from bread that has been slowly
dried in a preheated, very slow
oven and then crumbled)
300 g (10 oz) dried figs, chopped
1 tablespoon ground cinnamon
60 g (2 oz) butter
125 g (4 oz) dark (semisweet)
chocolate

SYRUP
2 cups (500 g/1 lb) sugar
2 cups (500 mL/16 fl oz) water
1 stick cinnamon
1 large strip of orange rind

TO ASSEMBLE THE DISH
250 g (8 oz) unsalted butter,
melted
whole cloves, for decoration

Serves 12-16

BAKLAVA IS SURELY Greece's most famous dessert. At Cosmos, we've taken it one step further and made a truly decadent version, which we serve with coffee. To make this baklava you will need a lot of patience and some spare time, but the results are well worth the effort. You will also need both a large surface area and a pasta-making machine.

Filo Pastry: Melt the chocolate in a double boiler. Set aside to cool.

Meanwhile, combine the flour and salt in a large bowl. Take the butter out of the freezer and grate into the flour with a vegetable grater. Rub the butter into the flour with your fingertips or a knife. Make a well in the centre and add the egg, melted chocolate and ¾ cup (185 mL/6 fl oz) of the mineral water. Working from the centre, combine the flour with the liquid using a knife or spatula. Add the rest of the water as you mix. Knead the dough for about 5 minutes. Cover with plastic wrap (cling film) and chill in the freezer for 1 hour.

Chocolate Fig Filling: Combine the nuts, breadcrumbs, figs and cinnamon in a bowl. Melt the butter and chocolate in a double boiler and stir into the nut mixture. Set aside.

Syrup: Combine the sugar and water in a large saucepan. Bring to the boil. Add the cinnamon and orange rind, and simmer for 10 minutes. Allow to cool.

To Assemble the Dish: Preheat the oven to 230°C (450°F/gas mark 8). Lightly grease a 39 x 23 x 4 cm (15½ x 9 x 1¾ in.) rectangular baking pan. Make sure that you have a large surface area available and that the pasta-making machine is ready.

Remove the filo pastry dough from the freezer and cut into thick slices. Dust each slice with a little flour. Roll each dough slice through the pasta machine, using the narrowest gauge, until the dough is paper thin. Set each sheet of pastry aside, lightly dusting with flour, and keep covered with a cloth while you prepare the rest of the dough.

Place enough sheets of filo side by side to cover the bottom of the baking pan, overlapping each sheet a little. Brush with the melted butter and repeat this process until you have three layers of pastry. Spread half of the Chocolate Fig Filling over the pastry layer.

Cover the filling with two layers of filo pastry, overlapping and brushing with butter as before. Now cover with the remaining Chocolate Fig Filling. Finally layer with the remaining sheets of filo (brushing each layer with butter) until all the filo is used. Cut away the excess filo hanging over the sides of the pan.

Using a sharp knife, carefully cut the baklava into rows of diamond-shaped portions, and stud the top of each diamond with a whole clove. Brush the surface of the filo with the remaining butter.

Bake in the oven for 5 minutes. Reduce the heat to 180°C (350°F/gas mark 4) and continue to bake for another 55 minutes, until golden. Remove the baklava from the oven and turn the oven off. Pour the cooled syrup over the top of the baklava. Return to the oven and let sit for another 30 minutes. Serve slices of baklava either warm with thick cream or cold with strong Greek coffee.

MASTIC AND RASPBERRY ICE CREAM WITH RED FRUITS IN ROSE-WATER SYRUP

Pagoto me Mastiha ke Kokina Frouta me Anthonero

MASTIC AND RASPBERRY
    ICE CREAM
*1 vanilla bean (pod), cut in half
    lengthwise*
*4 cups (1 L/1¾ imp. pts) thickened
    (heavy, double) cream*
10 egg yolks
*1¼ cups (250 g/8 oz) caster
    (superfine) sugar plus 5 g
    (⅙ oz) mastic ground with
    1 tablespoon of the sugar*
*250 g (8 oz) raspberries, fresh
    or frozen*

RED FRUITS IN ROSE-WATER
    SYRUP
*250 g (8 oz) red fruits of your
    choice (such as strawberries,
    cherries, sliced blood (purple)
    plums, etc.)*
1 cup (250 mL/8 fl oz) water
1 cup (250 g/8 oz) sugar
1 tablespoon lemon juice
1 tablespoon rose-water

Serves 8-10

MASTIC IS A RESINOUS GUM produced by a shrub that grows on the island of Chios, the supposed birthplace of Homer. In Greece, mastic is used to flavour a liqueur called *mastiha*. History notes that mastic was the original sugar-free, non-chemical chewing gum.

Mastic and Raspberry Ice Cream: Scrape the seeds out of the vanilla bean into a saucepan. Add the cream and bring to just below boiling point. Remove from the heat.

Beat the egg yolks and caster sugar together until pale and creamy. Slowly add the scalded cream, whisking all the time. Return to the saucepan and stir over a moderate heat until the mixture coats the back of a spoon. Pour into a stainless steel bowl and stir in the ground mastic. Chill the mixture until cold. Strain out the vanilla seeds and add the raspberries. Churn in a domestic icecream maker following the manufacturer's instructions.

Red Fruits in Rose-Water Syrup: Bring the water, sugar and lemon juice to the boil. Simmer for 5 minutes then add the rose-water. Remove from the heat and cool the syrup completely. Pour over the red fruits and chill in the refrigerator until needed.

To Serve: Serve the Mastic and Raspberry Ice Cream either in a pool of Red Fruits in Rose-Water Syrup or with the fruits and their syrup poured over the top.

GREEK COFFEE
AND WALNUT ICE CREAM CAKE

Pagoto me Kafe ke Karidia

WALNUT CAKE

1½ cups (250 g/8 oz) walnuts,
*   finely ground*
½ cup (125 g/4 oz) sugar
2 teaspoons ground cinnamon
5 egg whites (reserve the yolks for
*   the ice cream)*
pinch of cream of tartar

ICE CREAM

1 vanilla bean (pod), cut in half
*   lengthwise*
4 cups (1 L/1¾ imp. pts) thickened
*   (heavy, double) cream*
2 scant teaspoons Greek-style coffee
10 egg yolks
1¼ cups (250 g/8 oz) caster
*   (superfine) sugar*
1¼ cups (150 g/5 oz) roughly
*   chopped toasted walnuts*

Serves 8-10

GROWING UP IN a Greek household, you come to learn that coffee is more than a drink. In fact, it's almost a pastime; family and friends get together over a cup of coffee and a glass of water to share jokes, gossip and heated debate about marriage, life and politics.

When my father makes Greek coffee, he never makes it for one. There's always someone around who wants to share a cup with him, and if no one's around, 'Well,' he says, 'I'll just have to have two.'

Walnut Cake: Preheat the oven to 160°C (325°F/gas mark 3). Grease a Swiss roll cake pan. Line with silicon paper (baking parchment) and grease.

Combine the walnuts, sugar and cinnamon in a large bowl. Beat the egg whites with the cream of tartar until stiff. Gently fold into the nut mixture. Spread into the cake pan and bake for 15 minutes. Cool in the pan. Turn out and set aside.

Ice Cream: Cut the vanilla bean in half and scrape out the seeds. Heat the cream in a saucepan with the coffee and vanilla seeds to just below boiling point. Cover and set aside.

Whisk the egg yolks and caster sugar together until pale and creamy. Slowly add the cream mixture. Return to the pan and stir over a moderate heat until it coats the back of a spoon. Strain out the seeds and chill the mixture. Churn in a domestic icecream maker following the manufacturer's instructions. Add the walnuts at the last moment.

To Finish the Dish: Line a 6-cup (1.5 L/2½ imp. pt) loaf pan with silicon paper. Pour in half the ice cream and cover with the Walnut Cake, cut to the size of the loaf pan. Gently cover with the remaining ice cream and freeze for at least 6 hours. Serve cut into slices.

ROCKMELON ICE WITH OUZO AND BERRIES

Piponi Pagoto me Ouzo ke Moures

1¼ cups (300 g/10 oz) sugar
1¼ cups (300 mL/10 fl oz) water
1 kg (2 lb) ripe fresh rockmelon
    (cantaloupe, ogen melon) pulp
juice of 1 lemon
1 teaspoon orange blossom water
250 g (8 oz) summer berries of
    your choice (such as blackberries
    and blueberries)
ouzo, as needed

Serves 6-8

IN THE MIDDLE OF SUMMER in almost any *ouzerie* or taverna on the islands of Greece, someone is enjoying a plate of rockmelon (cantaloupe) and a shot of ouzo.

Ouzo is a spirit made by distilling the pulp that is left after grapes have been crushed for wine. It is then flavoured with anise.

Ices are also very popular among tourists and natives of Greece alike, and with this in mind I created what I believe is *the* perfect summer dessert.

Bring the sugar and water to the boil in a large saucepan. Add the rockmelon pulp and lemon juice, and simmer for 5 minutes. Remove from the heat and stir in the orange blossom water. Chill the mixture until cold. Freeze in an icecream maker following the manufacturer's instructions.

When ready to serve, scoop the ice into serving dishes, top with some berries and pour a shot of ouzo over each serving at the last moment.

INDEX